Stitch and de-stress with 40 Simple Patterns

CROSS-STITCH TO CALM

Leah Lintz

INTERWEAVE
interweave.com

Smile
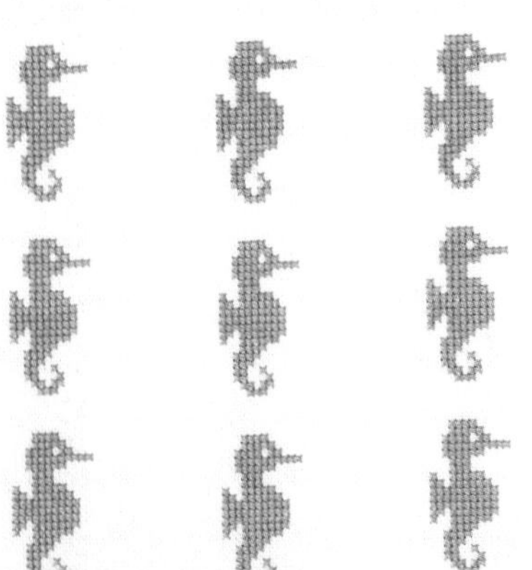

Contents

Introduction

I have always called cross-stitch "my therapy" and over the years have realized it's not just *my* therapy, it's widespread! It's a simple craft that keeps your hands busy but allows your mind to chill out.

My one frustration was due to a lack of cross-stitch patterns that suited my personal style. Frilly and cutesy are not to my taste! So I started to make my own patterns in a more bold, cheerful, graphic style, reflecting the themes that I adore--from the natural world (flowers, plants, animals) to keyphrases that reflect the best that life has to offer ("family" and "eat," among others!)

Simple patterns look fabulous and elegant on your walls; and as a bonus, they don't take long to stitch. Most of the patterns in this book can be easily completed in a weekend. Also, colors can be simply changed to match your own stylish interiors.

So, cozy up and stitch away! You've got lots of empty canvas to fill!

Eat.

Tools & Materials

Cross-stitch is a simple craft involving fabric, thread, and a needle. Add a simple and pleasing pattern, and you have a relaxing and inexpensive hobby. Most of the patterns in this book have interchangeable colors that can be substituted to suit your taste and/or your stash of thread and fabric.

EMBROIDERY FLOSS ↓

Each pattern in this book lists the relevant colors needed to complete each project. DMC 6-stranded thread is the chosen brand of thread used for this book and is the most widely available. When stitching, it is advisable to use an 18-inch (45.5 cm) or shorter length of thread, to avoid tangles and knots.

Only two strands of the 6-stranded thread are needed for the projects in this book. Separation of the thread is achieved by gently rolling the end of thread in-between your thumb and finger. This will separate the threads, and the two threads needed can be pulled gently away and threaded into the needle.

NEEDLES →

Tapestry needles are blunt and have a large(ish) eye, making it easier to thread your strands.

Tapestry needles range in size, but for the purposes of this book, you only need one! All of the projects in this book require a size 26 needle.

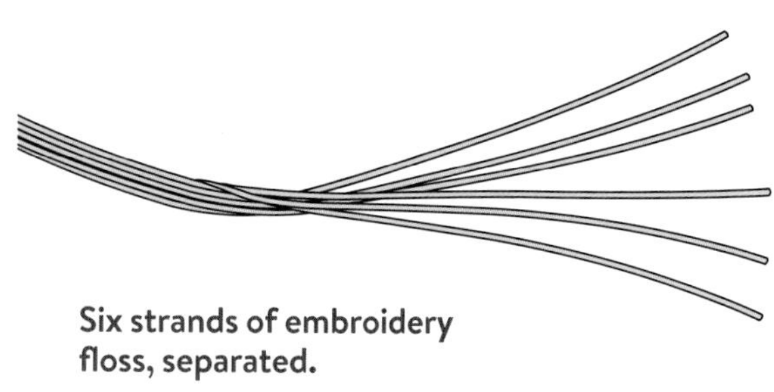

Six strands of embroidery floss, separated.

HPI, Gauge, & Count

HPI stands for holes per inch and also refers to the gauge or "count" of the fabric. The most popular cross-stitch fabric is 14-count, which means you will have 14 holes per linear inch. 18-count has 18 holes per inch, and so on. Therefore, the higher the count, the smaller the weave.

All of of the projects in this book have been stitched on 28-count evenweave fabric, but over two holes instead of one. As a result, even though the weave of the fabric is smaller, the resulting designs are equivalent in size to those done on 14-count fabric.

FABRIC →

Cross-stitch fabric is readily available at local craft supply stores and can be as inexpensive as $2.99 for 12" × 18" (30.5 × 45.5 cm) of fabric.

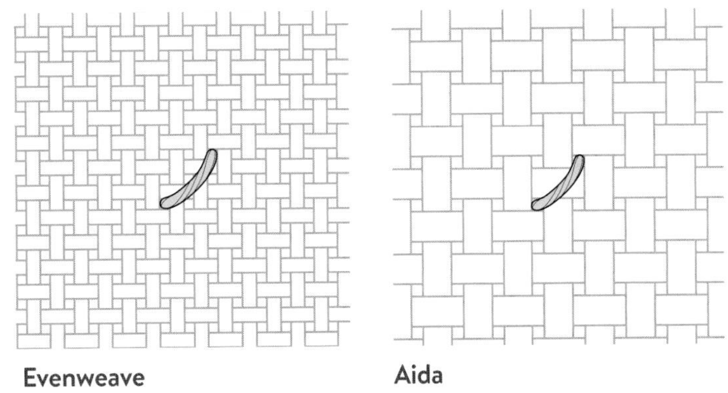

Evenweave   Aida

Evenweave

Evenweave fabric is fabric in which there are the same number of threads across the warp as across the weft. Generally, evenweave fabric is woven with a single thread; and when cross-stitching, two holes or threads need to be stitched across.

Aida

Aida is the most popular evenweave fabric for cross-stitch. This fabric is woven with threads grouped into bundles, forming little spaces that are easy to see.

Aida is great for beginners, as the fibers are specially woven to create a square grid which is easily visible.

Linen

Linen is a gorgeous fabric to look at once a project is stitched, but a bit more challenging for a beginner, as the fibers are closer together (28-count or 32-count) and therefore harder to see correctly (well, at least for this aging stitcher!).

EMBROIDERY HOOP →

An embroidery hoop can be a useful tool for keeping your fabric taut while stitching. It's not essential, though; even if you don't use one, the fabric will still stay even as you stitch.

Hoops are also a great tool for displaying the finished piece. Just nail a hole in the wall and hang it right up!

STARTING YOUR PROJECT

Reading your chart

Each square of your chart represents one complete cross-stitch and contains a symbol and color that corresponds to the thread color in the accompanying symbol/color key.

Working the chart

It's advisable to start working from the center of the chart and fabric so that your finished project is centered. Each pattern comes with a suggested amount of fabric to ensure you have at least 2" (5 cm) all the way around the piece for finishing.

1. Find the center of your chart: Black triangles are on the top and left side of your chart. You can find the center of the chart by extending lines outward from the triangles and observing where they intersect.
2. Find the center of your fabric. An easy way to find the center of your fabric is to fold the fabric in half vertically and pinch along the fold. Unfold the fabric. Next, fold your fabric horizontally and pinch along the fold. Open the fabric up and the two pinched folds will cross in the middle of your fabric.
3. When beginning to stitch, leave a 1" (2.5 cm) tail on the back of the fabric and hold it against the back as you stitch the next 4 or 5 stitches over the tail, securing your thread (**Figure 1**). This avoids the use of knots, which can show through and ruin the look of your project. When the color is complete or new thread is needed, weave your needle back through the last 4 or 5 stitches and clip the thread.

Figure 1

HALF-STITCH →

Bring your needle from the back of the cross-stitch fabric at position **1** and push it back through position **2**.

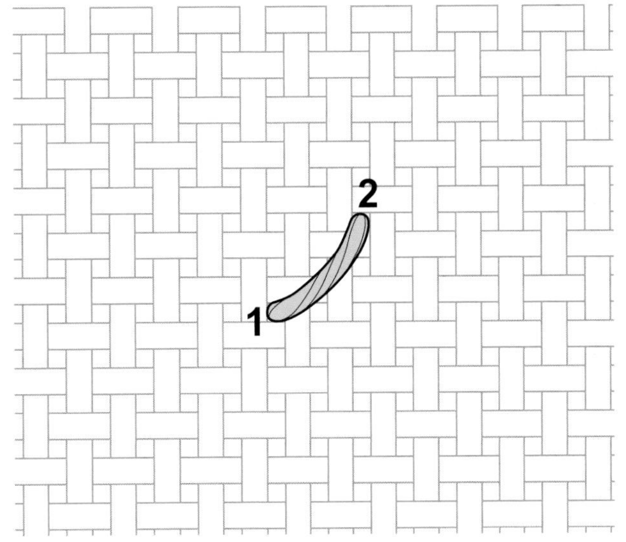

QUARTER-STITCH →

There are very few quarter-stitches used in the projects in this book. Quarter-stitches are mainly used to create a smoother and more rounded effect. The stitch is created by stitching only half the length of the half-stitch. The quarter-stitch can be stitched in any corner of the square normally reserved for a full cross-stitch.

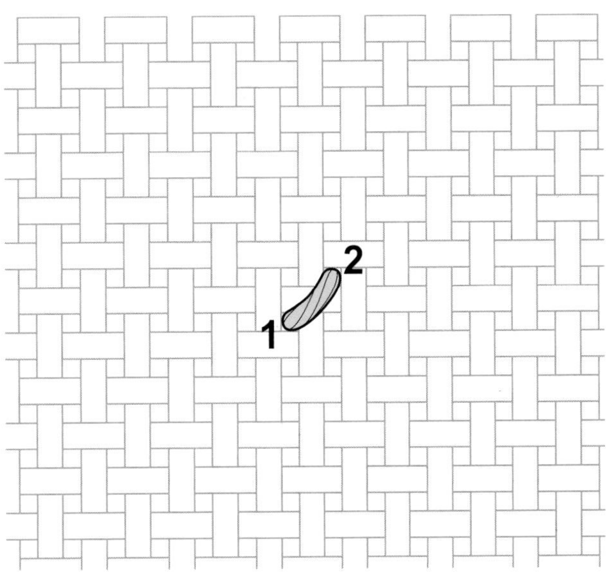

STITCHING A HORIZONTAL ROW↘

1. Bring your needle from the back of the cross-stitch fabric at position **1** and push it back through position **2**, then up at **3** and down at **4**.
2. Repeat this step until you have the required number of half-stitches for the horizontal row (**Figure 1**).
3. Complete the cross-stitch by bringing the needle from the back of the fabric through position **9** of the last half-stitch and push into position **10** (**Figure 2**) and repeat until all the half-stitches have been crossed.

In order to achieve a uniform look it's important to make sure that all the Xs are crossed in the same direction.

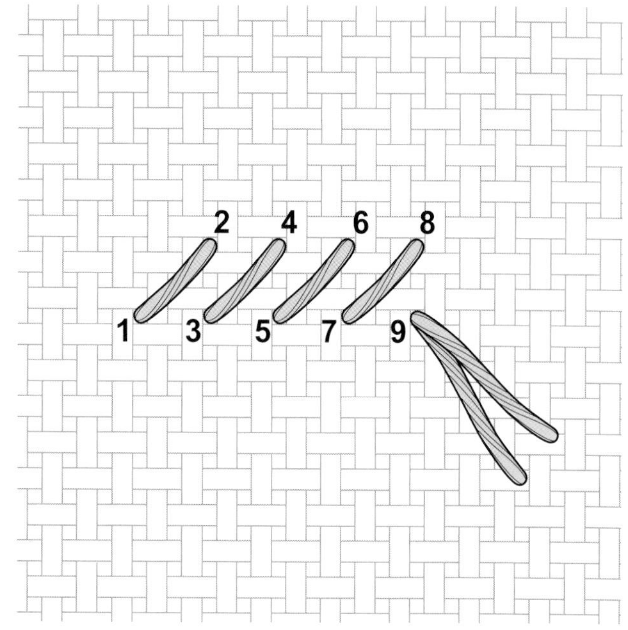

Figure 1

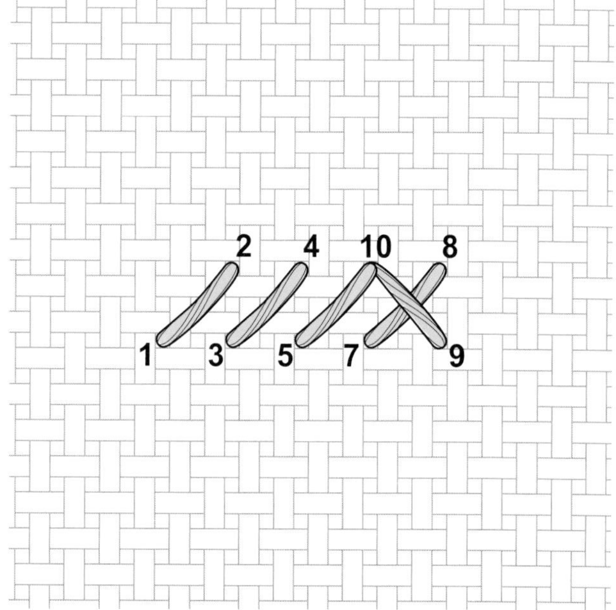

Figure 2

STITCHING A VERTICAL ROW↘

1. Bring your needle from the back of the cross-stitch fabric at position **1** and push it back through position **2**.
2. Repeat this step in the adjacent holes below until you have the required number of half-stitches for the vertical row (**Figure 1**).
3. Complete the cross-stitch by bringing the needle from the back of the fabric through position **9** (bottom) of the last half cross-stitch and push into position **10** (**Figure 2**) until all the half-stitches have been crossed.

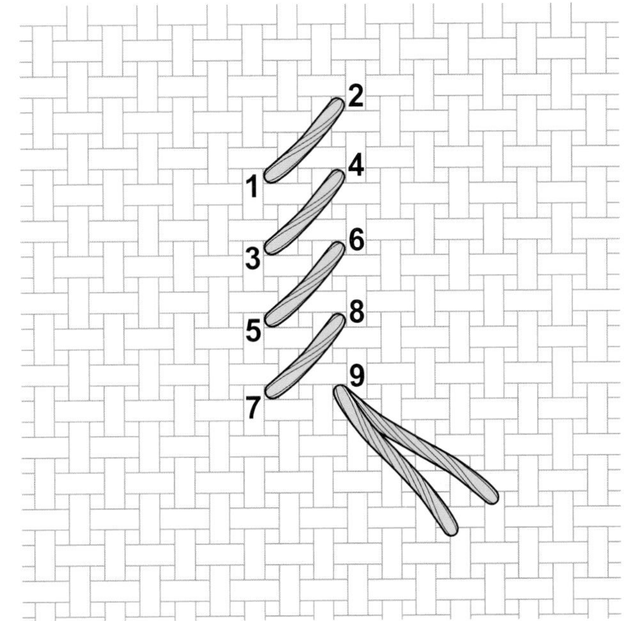

Figure 1

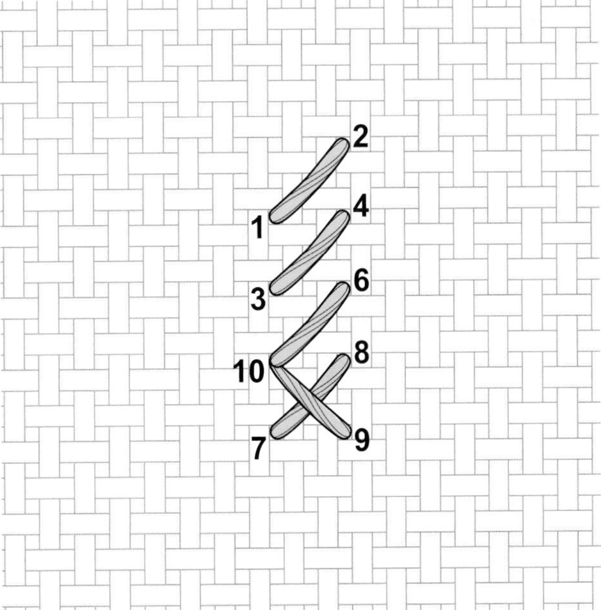

Figure 2

BACKSTITCH ↓

Backstitching is a running stitch (not an X) used to outline or create finer detail. This normally requires one less strand of floss for backstitching than you use for cross-stitching.

1. Start with your needle behind the fabric and push your needle through at the spot in which you wish to begin your backstitch line (**1**). Stitch one square ahead in the direction of the line (**2**).
2. Pull the needle through to the back of the fabric and push it up ahead one square (**3**). You are creating a line on the front and the back of your project.
3. Bring the needle back down at (**2**) and up again one square ahead of the stitching (**4**).
4. Bring the needle back down at (**3**) and up again one square ahead of the stitching (**5**).
5. Bring the needle back down at (**4**) and up again one square ahead of the stitching (**6**).

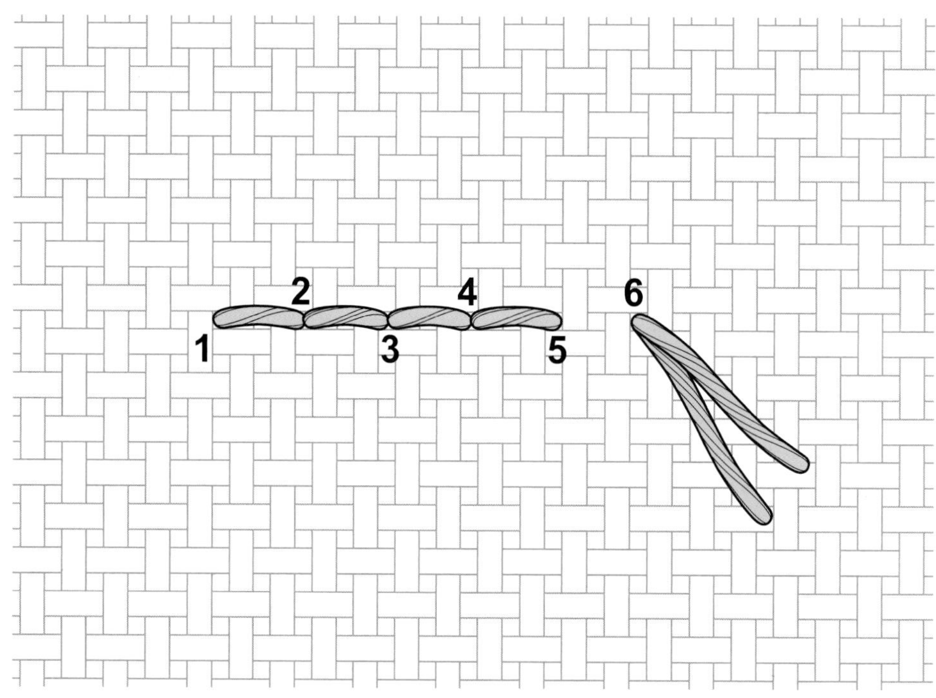

FINISHING

This book is called *Cross-Stitch to Calm*, and therefore, the appropriately easy finishing method should apply.

If you're a purist cross-stitcher, then by all means please use your tried and tested methods. I have tried the traditional method of mounting projects using the lacing method, and it works—but by golly, it's time-consuming!

My recommended method is to mount a piece on matboard. Double-sided tape is an awesome product to use adhere your cloth to the board, but just make sure the tape you're using is acid-free.

1. Prepare your finished piece by pressing with an iron. Place a cloth in between the iron and your work to avoid scorching your finished piece.
2. Trim your work to make sure that once it's adhered to the matboard, there is sufficient space around the board (wrong side) to attach the backboard using double-sided tape.
3. Place double-sided tape around the wrong side of the matboard's window.
4. Place your cross-stitched piece face up on a flat surface and center the matboard (tape side down) over your work. Place the matboard on top of your work. Once you're happy with the positioning, rub along all the edges of the window to ensure that your work is adhered. Repositioning is fairly easy; just peel your work off of the matboard (be careful not to the bend the board!) and reposition.
5. Place strips of tape around the matboard's edges (again, on the wrong side) and attach the backboard.
6. SMILE! Your lovingly made piece of cross-stitch is mounted!

Note that in all patterns, the fabric requirement allows for an extra 2" (5 cm) all around the design, for finishing.

CREATURES

Legend:
DMC-White

Bird on a Branch

✖✖✖✖✖✖✖✖✖✖✖

Thread:

DMC White (.4 skeins).

Stitch count:
100 × 138.

Design shown:
28-count evenweave over 2 threads, 7⅛" × 9⅞" (18.2 × 25.2 cm).

Fabric amount:
11½" × 14½" (29 × 37 cm).

Other fabrics:
16-count over 1 thread:
6¼" × 8⅝" (16 × 21.7 cm).
Suggested fabric amount:
11" × 13" (28 × 33 cm).

18-count over 1 thread:
5½" × 7⅝" (14 × 19.3 cm).
Suggested fabric amount:
10" × 12" (25.5 × 30.5 cm).

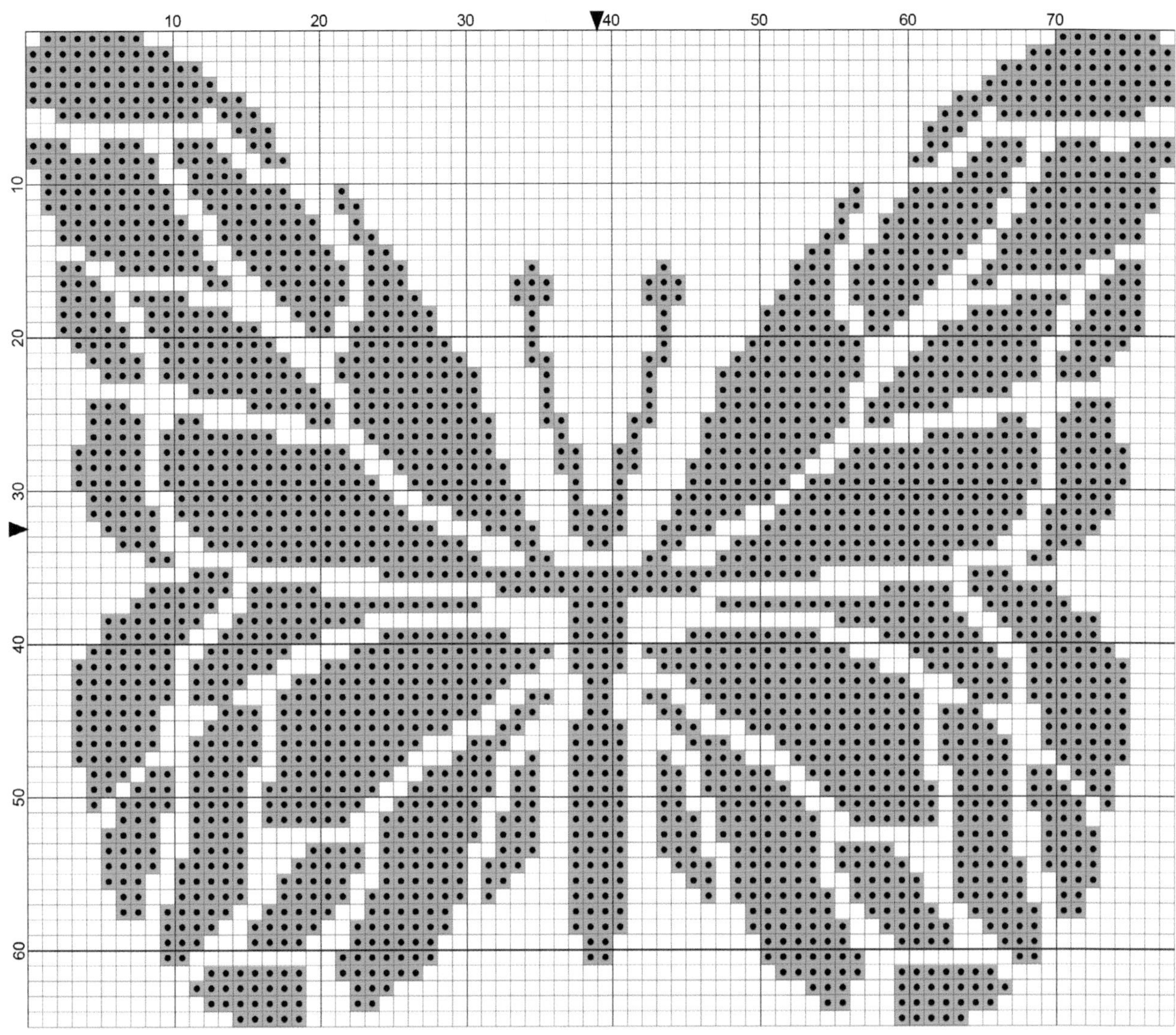
10
20
30
40
50
60
70
10
20
30
40
50
60
Legend:
DMC-352

Butterfly

Thread:
DMC 352 Light Coral (1 skein).

Stitch count:
78 × 65.

Design shown:
28-count evenweave over 2 threads, 5⅝" × 4⅝" (14.3 × 11.7 cm).

Fabric amount:
10" × 9" 25.5 × 23 cm).

Other fabrics:
16-count over 1 thread: 4⅞" × 4⅛" (12.4 × 10.5 cm). *Suggested fabric amount:* 9½" × 8½" (24 × 21.5 cm).

18-count over 1 thread: 4⅜" × 3⅝" (11.1 × 9.2 cm). *Suggested fabric amount:* 9" × 8" (23 × 20.5 cm).

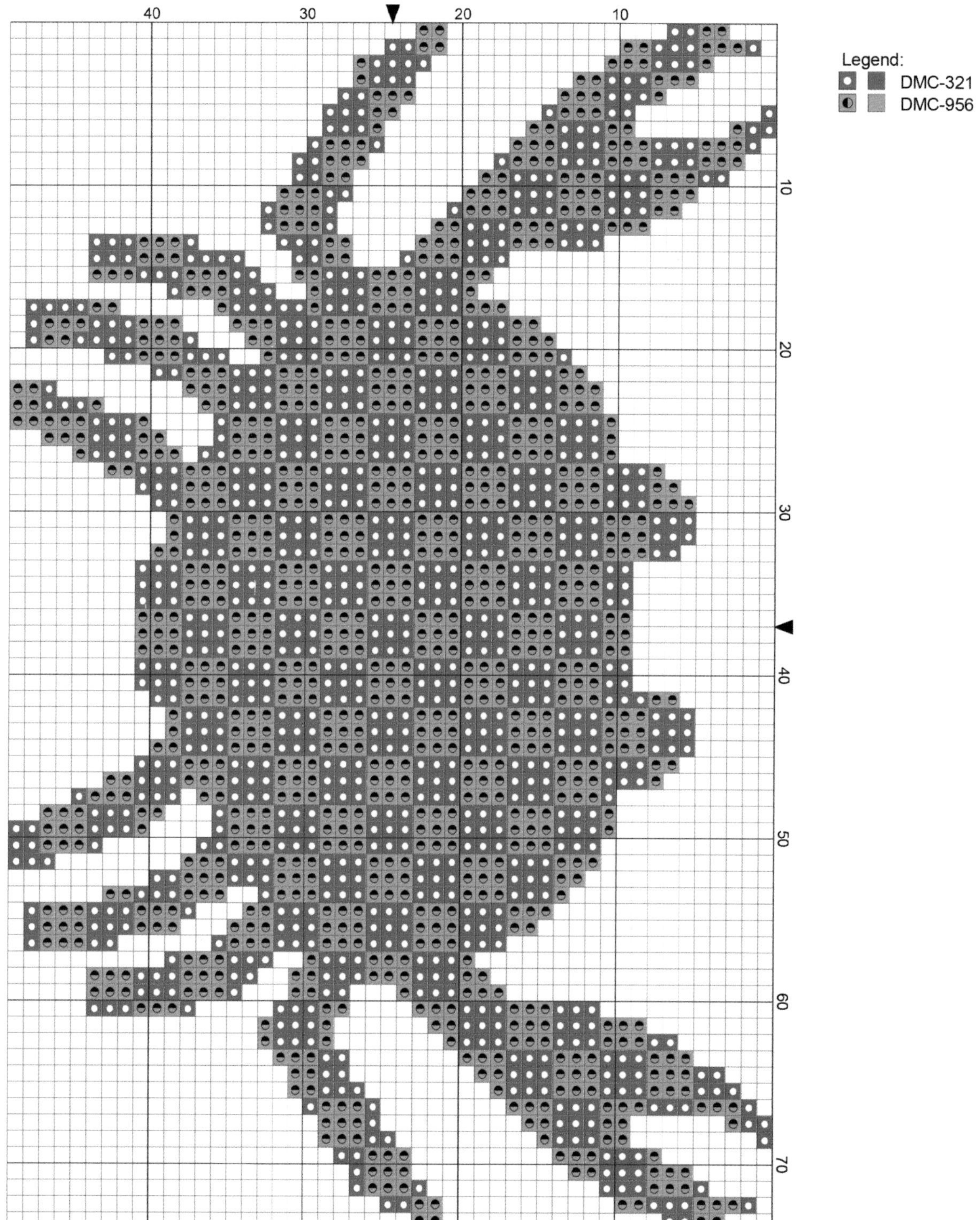

40
30
20
10
10
20
30
40
50
60
70
Legend:
DMC-321
DMC-956

Crab

Thread:
DMC 321 Christmas Red (.4 skeins).

DMC 956 Geranium(.4 skeins)

Stitch count:
74 × 49.

Design shown:
28-count evenweave over 2 threads, 5¼" × 3½" (13.5 × 9 cm).

Fabric amount:
10" × 8" (25.5 × 20.5 cm).

Other fabrics:
16-count over 1 thread: 4⅝" × 3⅛" (11.7 × 8 cm).
Suggested fabric amount: 9" × 7½" (23 × 19 cm).

18-count over 1 thread: 4⅛" × 2¾" (10.5 × 7 cm).
Suggested fabric amount: 8½" × 7" (21.5 × 18 cm).

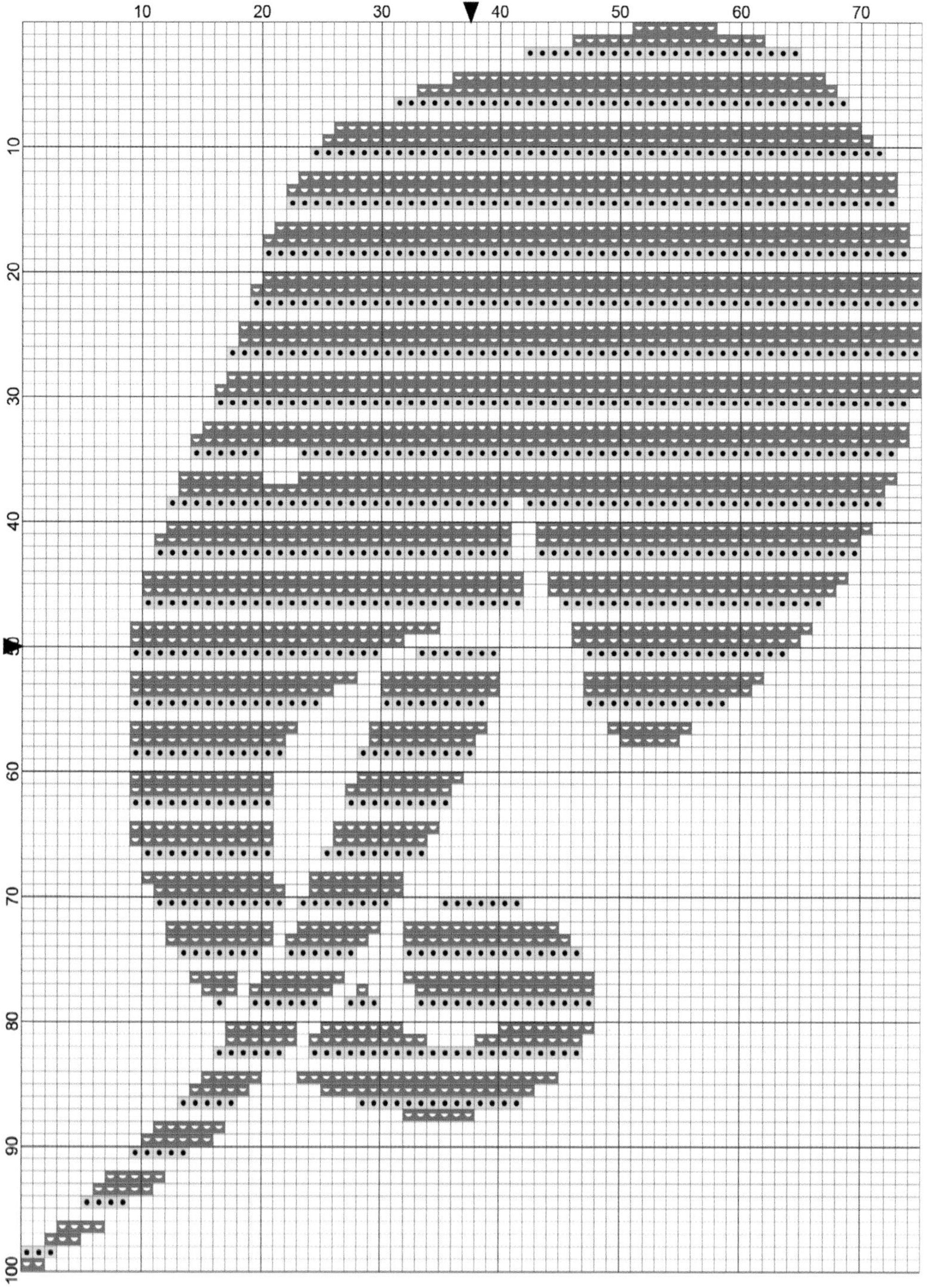

Legend:

DMC-451

DMC-453

Elephant

Thread:
DMC 451 Shell Gray, Dark (.4 skeins).

DMC 453 Shell Gray, Light (.4 skeins)

Stitch count:
75 × 100.

Design shown:
28-count evenweave over 2 threads, 5⅜" × 7⅛" (13.7 × 18.2 cm).

Fabric amount:
10" × 11½" (25.5 × 29 cm).

Other fabrics:
16-count over 1 thread: 4¾" × 6¼" (12 × 16 cm). *Suggested fabric amount:* 9" × 11" (23 × 28 cm).

18-count over 1 thread: 4⅛" × 5½" (10.5 × 14 cm). *Suggested fabric amount:* 8½" × 10" (21.5 × 25.5 cm).

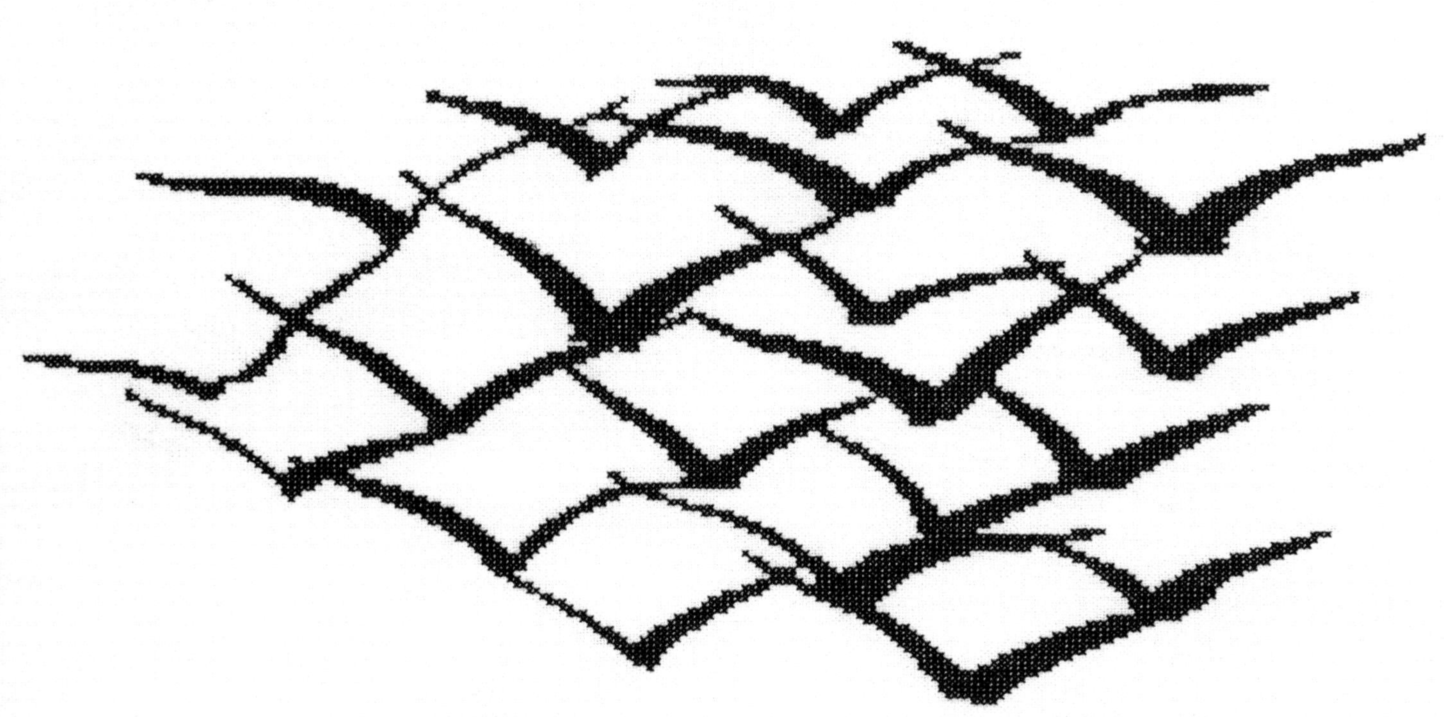

Flock

Thread:
DMC 310 Black (.7 skeins).

Stitch count:
199 × 117.

Design shown:
28-count evenweave over 2 threads, 14¼" × 8⅜" (36 × 21.3 cm).

Fabric amount:
18½" × 13" (47 × 33 cm).

Other fabrics:
16-count over 1 thread: 12½" × 7⅞" (31.5 × 18.7 cm).
Suggested fabric amount: 17" × 12" (43 × 30.5 cm).

18-count over 1 thread: 11" × 6½" (28 × 16.5 cm).
Suggested fabric amount: 15½" × 11" (39.5 × 28 cm).

Legend:
DMC-310

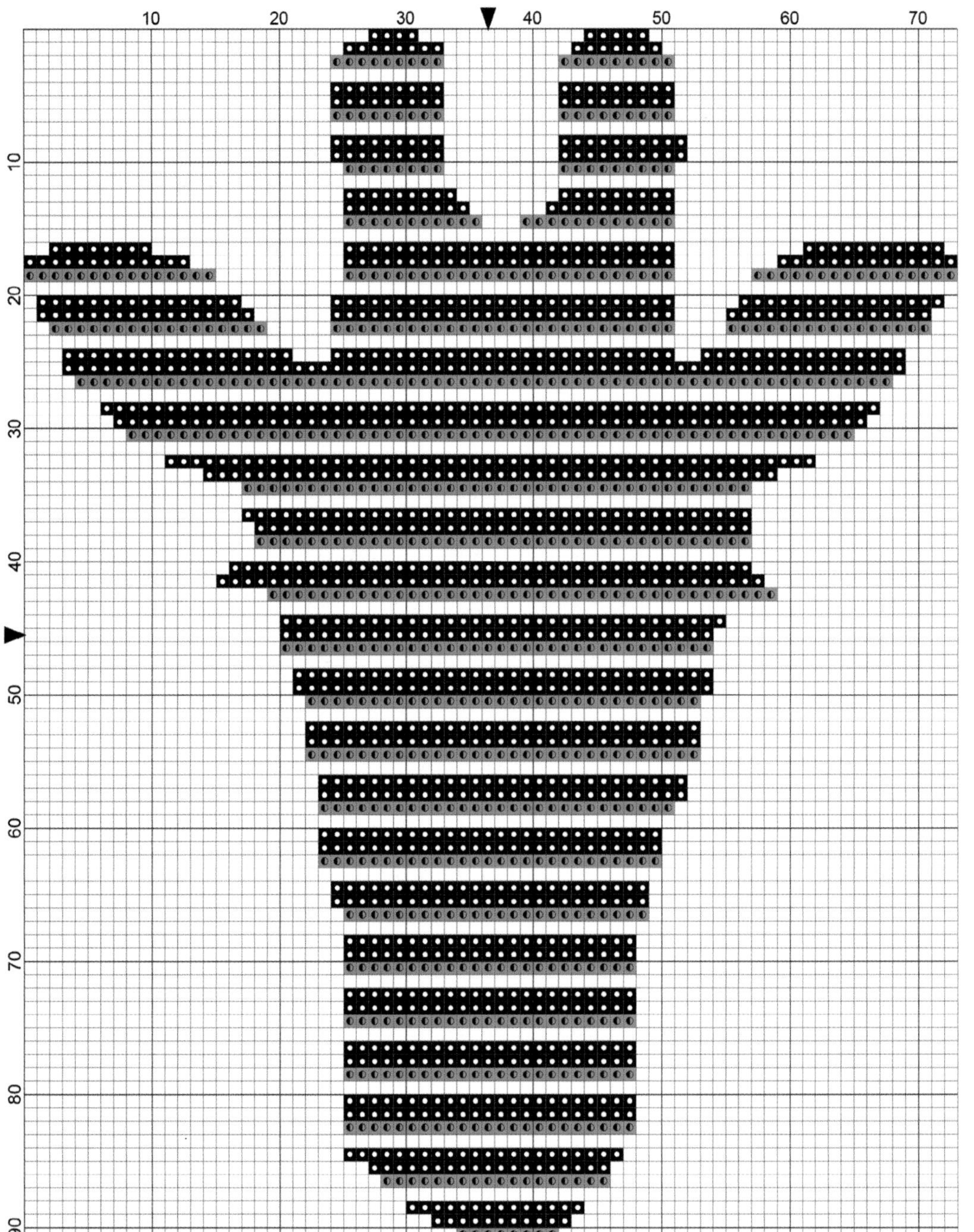

Legend:

DMC-310

DMC-647

Giraffe

Thread:
DMC 310 Black (.6 skeins).

DMC 647 Beaver Gray, Medium (.3 skeins).

Stitch count:
73 × 91.

Design shown:
28-count evenweave over 2 threads, 5¼" × 6½" (13.5 × 16.5 cm).

Fabric amount:
9½" × 11" (24 × 28 cm).

Other fabrics:
16-count over 1 thread: 4⅝" × 5¾" (11.7 × 14.5 cm).
Suggested fabric amount: 9" × 10" (23 × 25.5 cm).

18-count over 1 thread: 4" × 5" (10 × 12.5 cm).
Suggested fabric amount: 8½" × 9½" (21.5 × 24 cm).

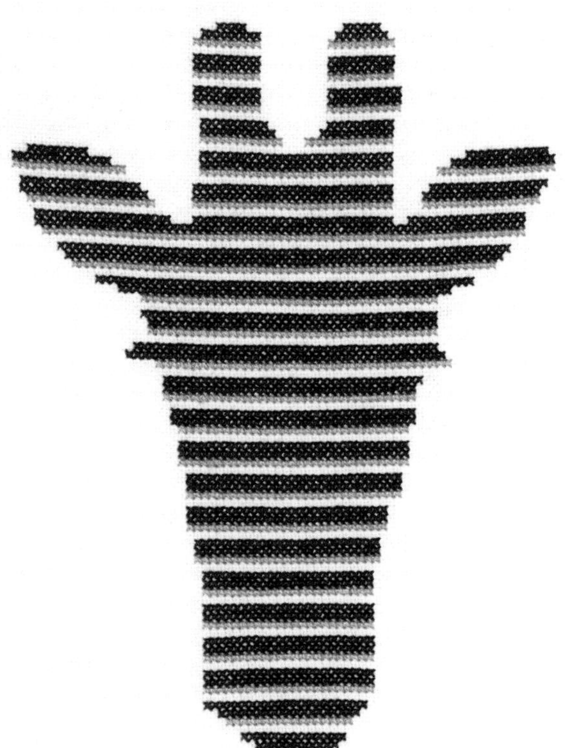

Legend:

DMC-993

Thread:
DMC 3022 Brown Gray, Medium (.6 skeins).

Stitch count:
46 × 90.

Design shown:
28-count evenweave over 2 threads,
3¼" × 6⅜" (8.5 × 16.2 cm).

Fabric amount:
8" × 11" (20.5 × 28 cm).

Other fabrics:
16-count over 1 thread: 2⅞" × 5⅝" (7.3 × 14.3 cm).
Suggested fabric amount: 7½" × 10" (19 × 25.5 cm).

18-count over 1 thread: 2½" × 5" (6.5 × 12.5 cm).
Suggested fabric amount: 7" × 9½" (18 × 24 cm).

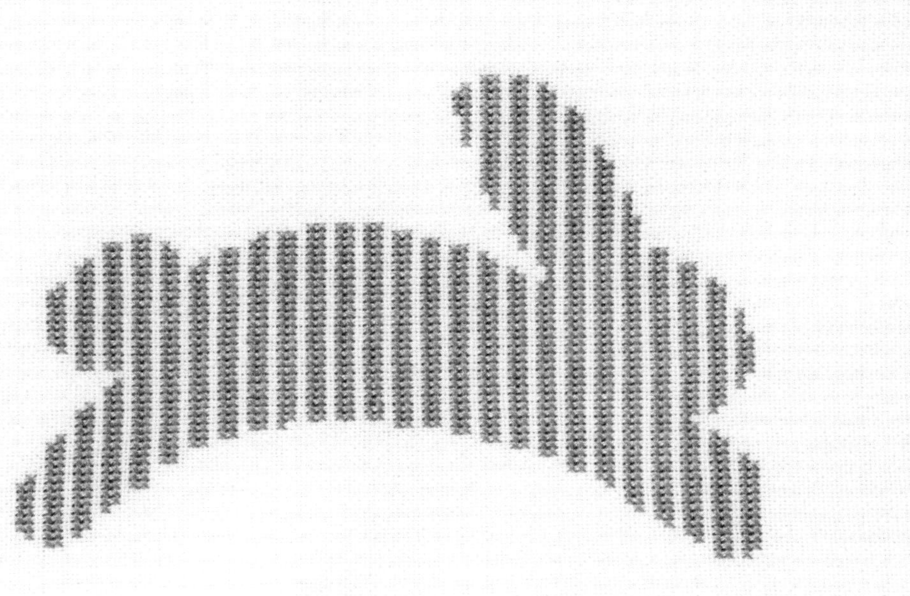

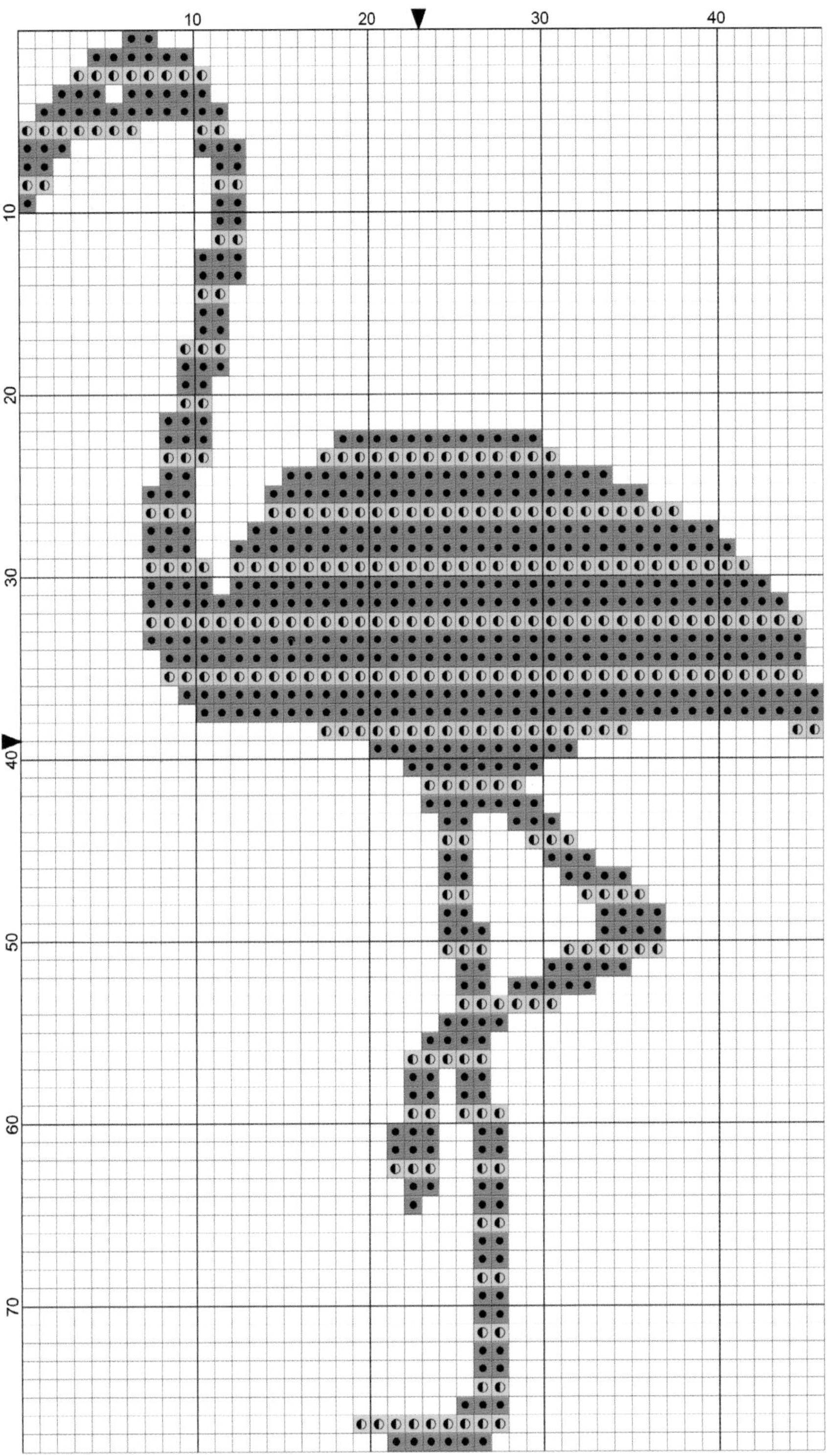

Legend:

DMC-3804

DMC-761

Pink Flamingo

Thread:
DMC 3804 Cyclamen Pink, Dark (.2 skeins).

DMC 761 Salmon, Light Dark (.1 skeins).

Stitch count:
46 × 78.

Design shown:
28-count evenweave over 2 threads, 3¼" × 5⅝" (8.5 × 14.3 cm).

Fabric amount:
8" × 10" (20.5 × 25.5 cm).

Other fabrics:
16-count over 1 thread:
2⅞" × 4⅞" (7.3 × 12.4 cm).
Suggested fabric amount:
7½" × 9½" (19 × 24 cm).

18-count over 1 thread:
2½" × 4⅜" (6.5 × 11.1 cm).
Suggested fabric amount:
7" × 9" (18 × 23 cm).

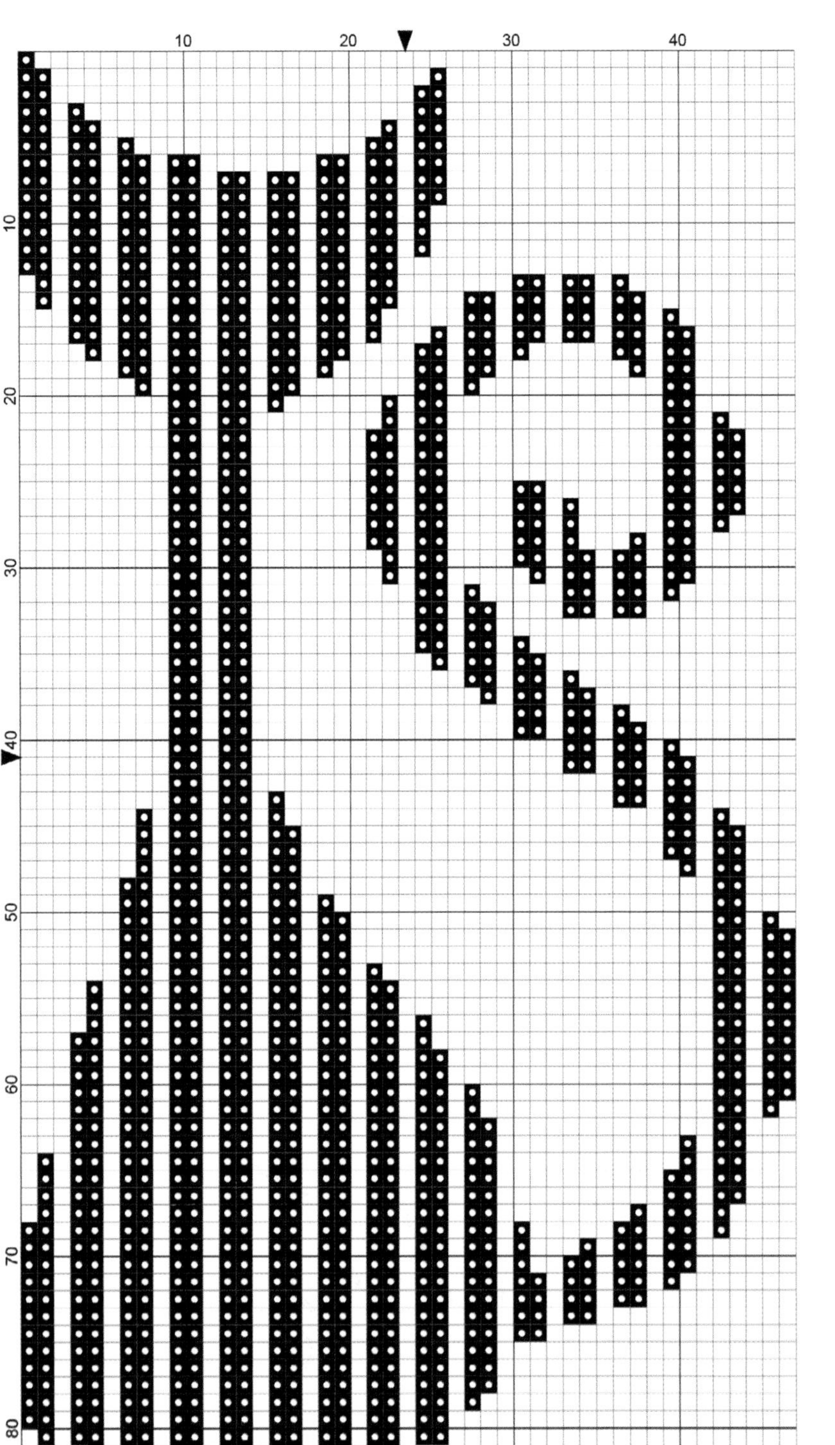

Legend:
DMC-310

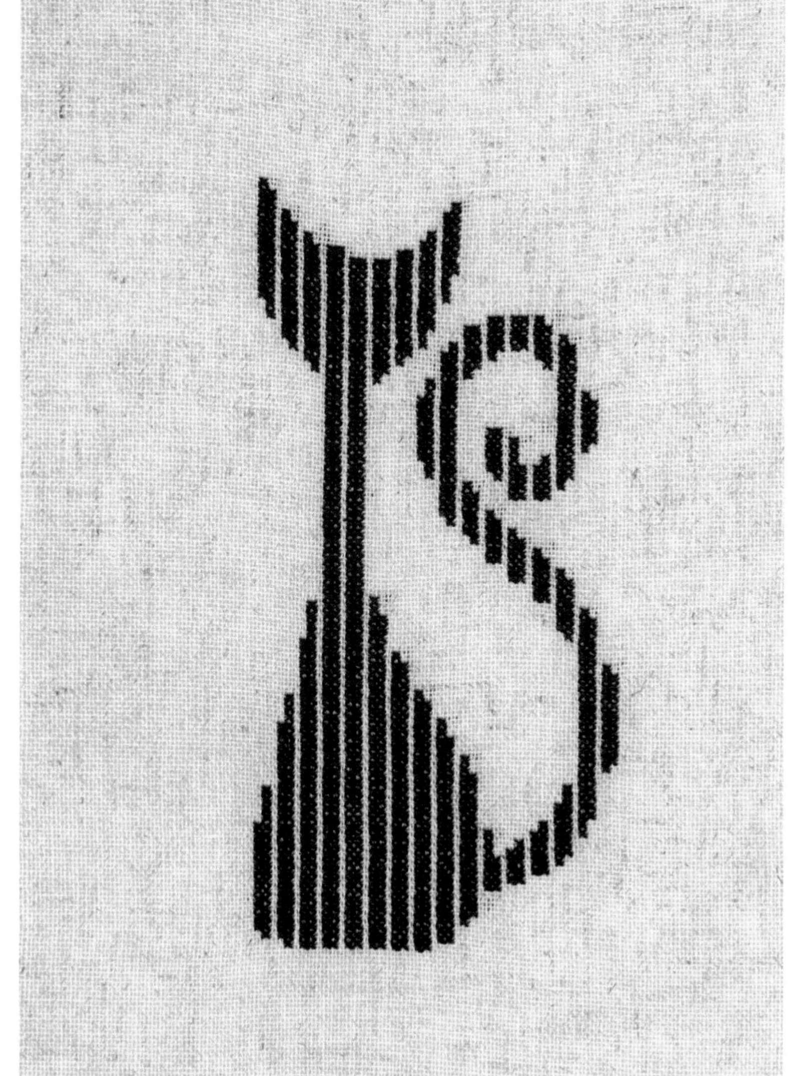

Thread:
DMC 310 Black
(.5 skeins).

Stitch count:
47 × 82.

Design shown:
28-count evenweave over
2 threads, 3⅜" × 5⅞"
(8.6 × 14.9 cm).

Fabric amount:
8" × 10½" (20.5 × 26.5 cm).

Other fabrics:
16-count over 1 thread:
3" × 5⅛" (7.5 × 13 cm).
Suggested fabric amount:
7½" × 9½" (19 × 24 cm).

18-count over 1 thread:
2⅝" × 4½" 6.7 × 11.5 cm).
Suggested fabric amount:
7" × 9" (18 × 23 cm).

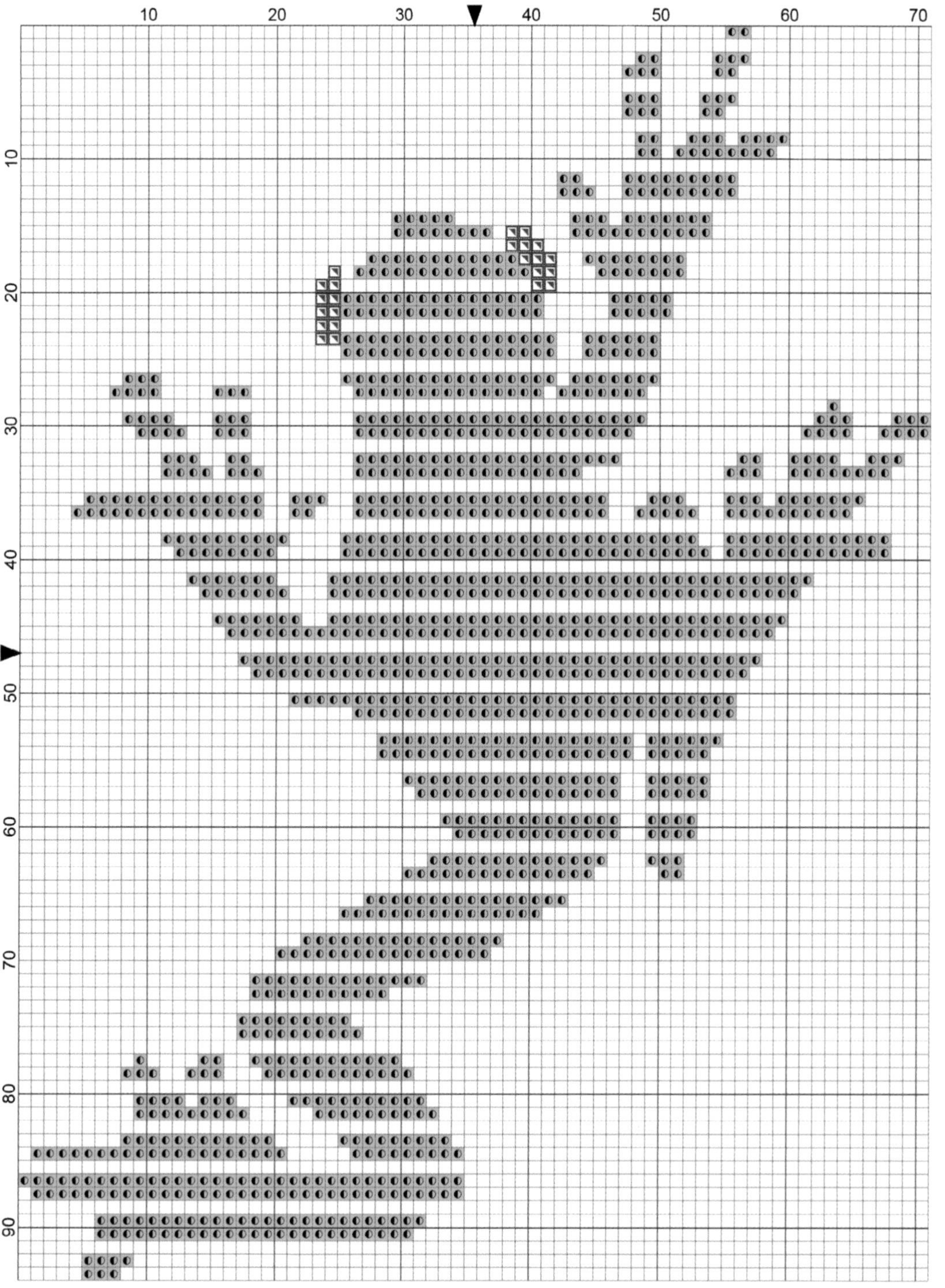
10
20
30
40
50
60
70
80
90
Legend:
DMC-704
DMC-498

Red-Eyed Tree Frog

Thread:
DMC 704 Chartreuse, Bright (.6 skeins).

DMC 498 Christmas Red, Dark (.1 skeins).

Stitch count:
71 × 94.

Design shown:
28-count evenweave over 2 threads, 5⅛" × 6¾" (13 × 17 cm).

Fabric amount:
9½" × 11" (24 × 28 cm).

Other fabrics:
16-count over 1 thread:
4½" × 5⅞" (11.5 × 14.9 cm).
Suggested fabric amount:
9" × 10½" (23 × 26.5 cm).

18-count over 1 thread:
4" × 5¼" (10 × 13.5 cm).
Suggested fabric amount:
8½" × 9½" (21.5 × 24 cm).

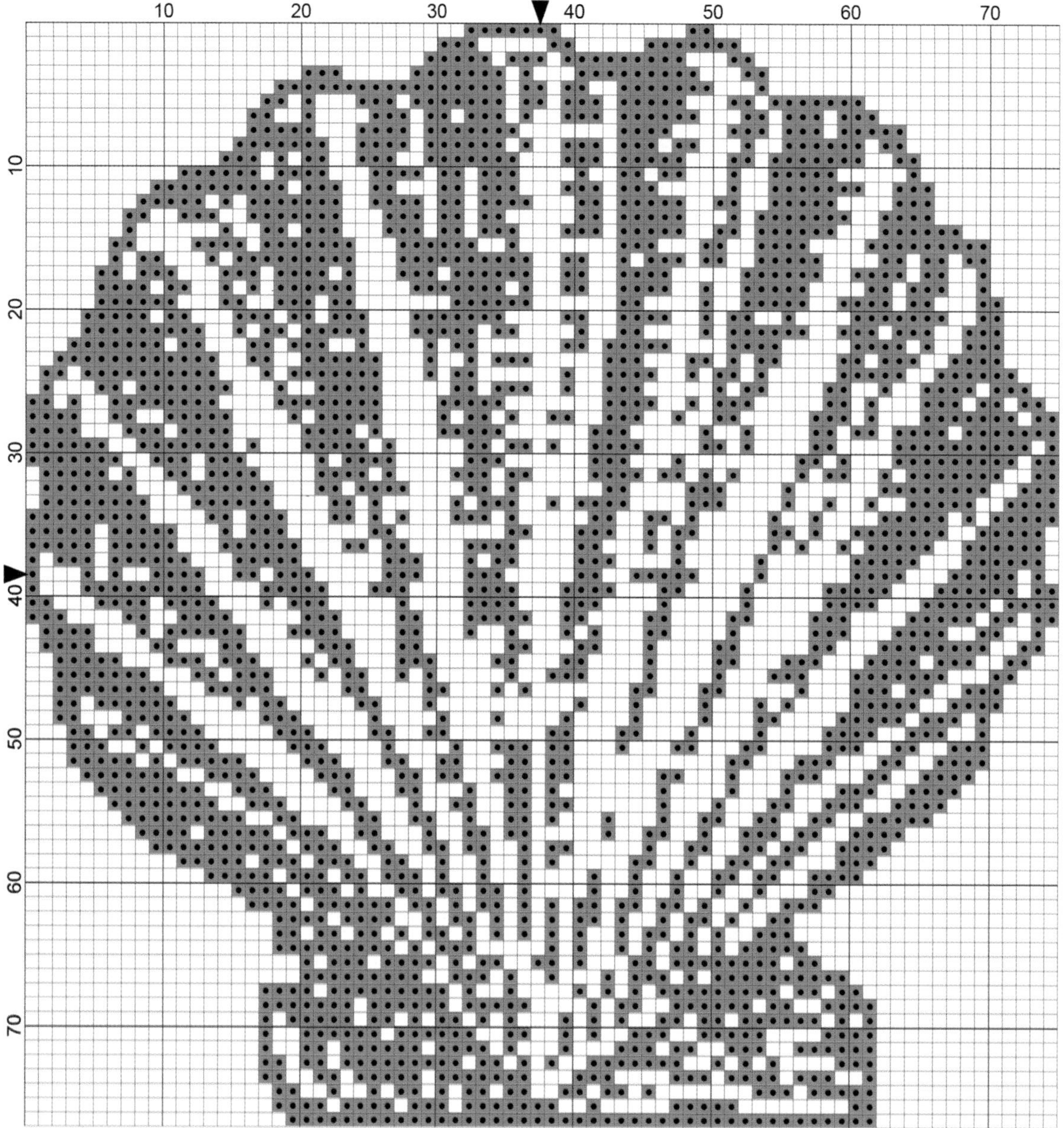

Legend:

DMC-169

Scallop Shell

Thread:
DMC 169 Pewter, Light (1 skein).

Stitch count:
75 × 77.

Design shown:
28-count evenweave over 2 threads, 5⅜" × 5½" (13.7 × 14 cm).

Fabric amount:
10" × 10" (25.5 × 25.5 cm).

Other fabrics:
16-count over 1 thread: 4¾" × 4⅞" (12 × 12.4 cm). *Suggested fabric amount:* 9" × 9½" (23 × 24 cm).

18-count over 1 thread: 4⅛" × 4¼" (10.5 × 11 cm). *Suggested fabric amount:* 8½" × 9" (21.5 × 23 cm).

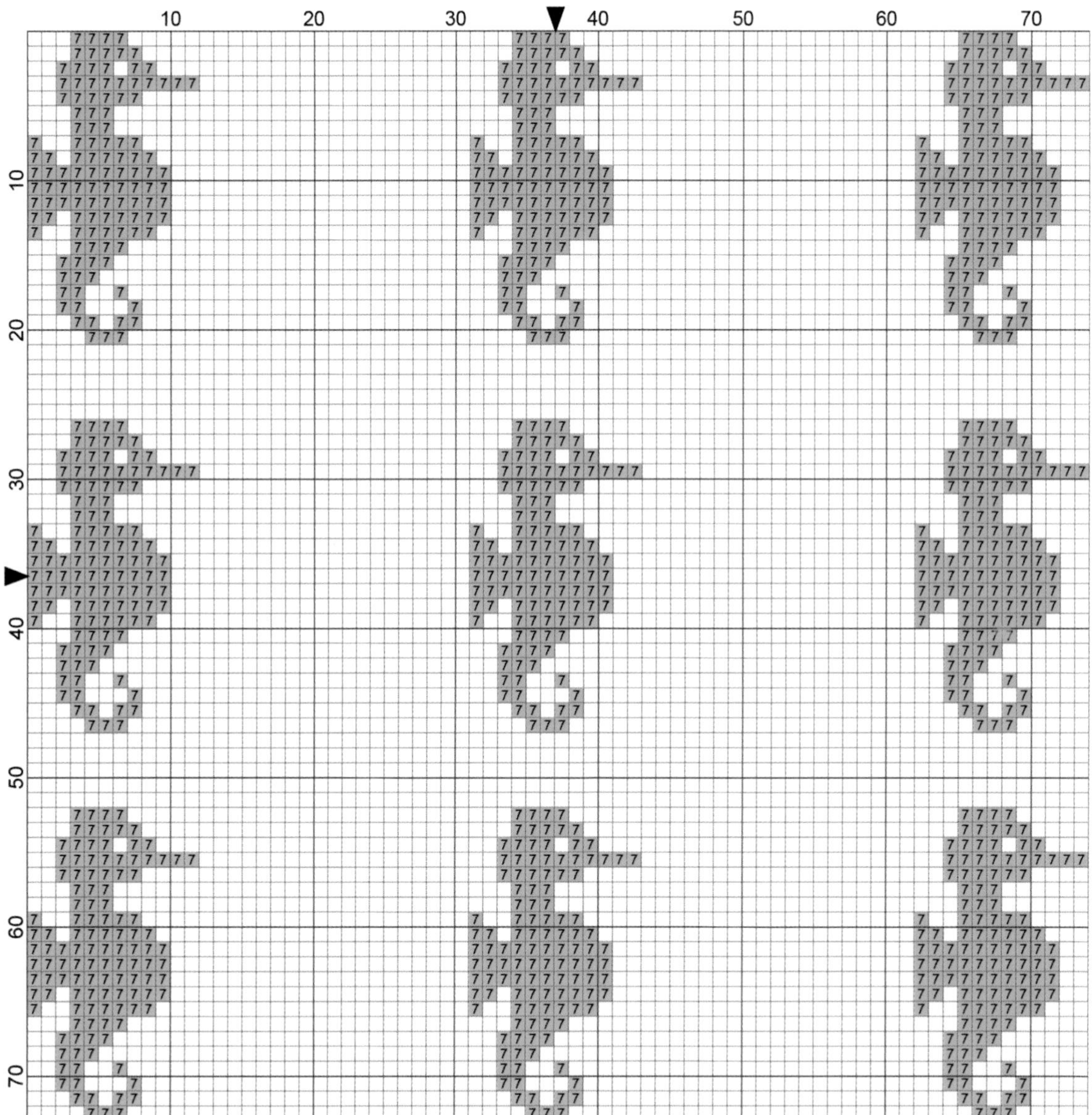

Legend:
7 DMC-3846

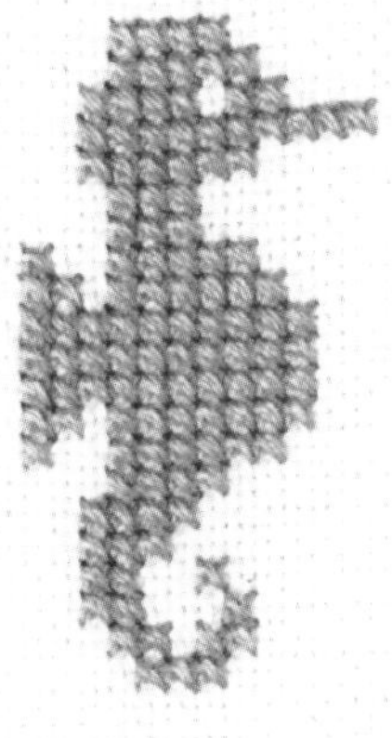

Seahorses

Thread:
DMC 3846 Bright Turquoise, Light (.4 skeins).

Stitch count:
74 × 73.

Design shown:
28-count evenweave over 2 threads,
5¼" × 5¼" (13.5 × 13.5 cm).

Fabric amount:
9½" × 9½" (24 × 24 cm).

Other fabrics:
16-count over 1 thread: 4⅝" × 4⅝" (11.7 × 11.7 cm).
Suggested fabric amount: 9" × 9" (23 × 23 cm).

18-count over 1 thread: 4⅛" × 4" (10.5 × 10.5 cm).
Suggested fabric amount: 8½" × 8½" (21.5 × 21.5 cm).

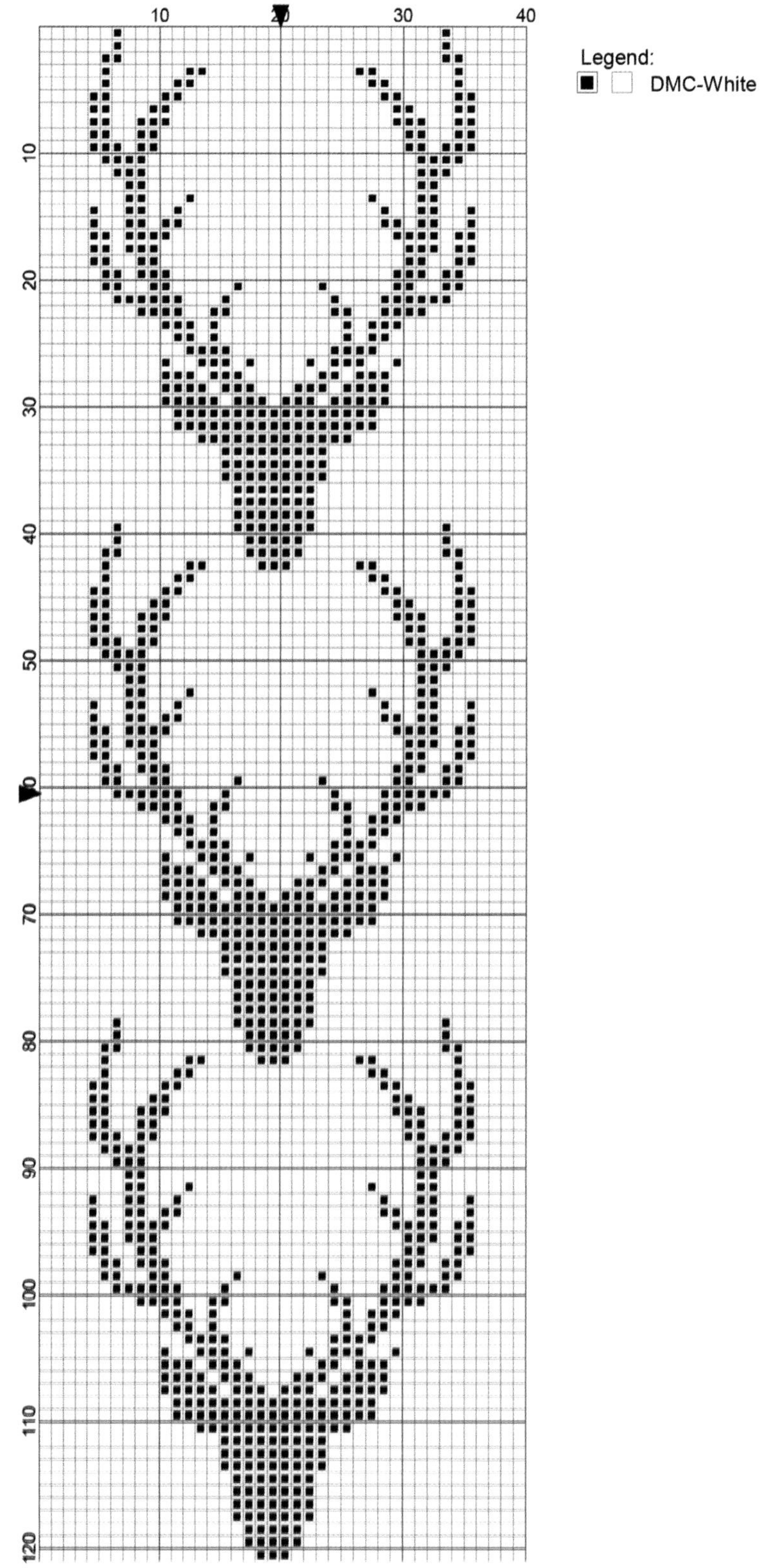
10
20
30
40
Legend:
DMC-White
10
20
30
40
50
60
70
80
90
100
110
120

Stag Heads

Thread:
DMC White (.5 skeins)

Stitch count:
40 × 121.

Design shown:
28-count evenweave over 2 threads, 2⅞" × 8⅝" (7.3 × 21.7 cm).

Fabric amount:
7½" × 13" (19 × 33 cm).

Other fabrics:
16-count over 1 thread: 2⅞" × 8⅝" (7.3 × 21.7 cm). *Suggested fabric amount:* 7" × 12" (18 × 30.5 cm).

18-count over 1 thread: 2¼" × 6¾" (7 × 17 cm). *Suggested fabric amount:* 6½" × 11" (16.5 × 28 cm).

NATURE

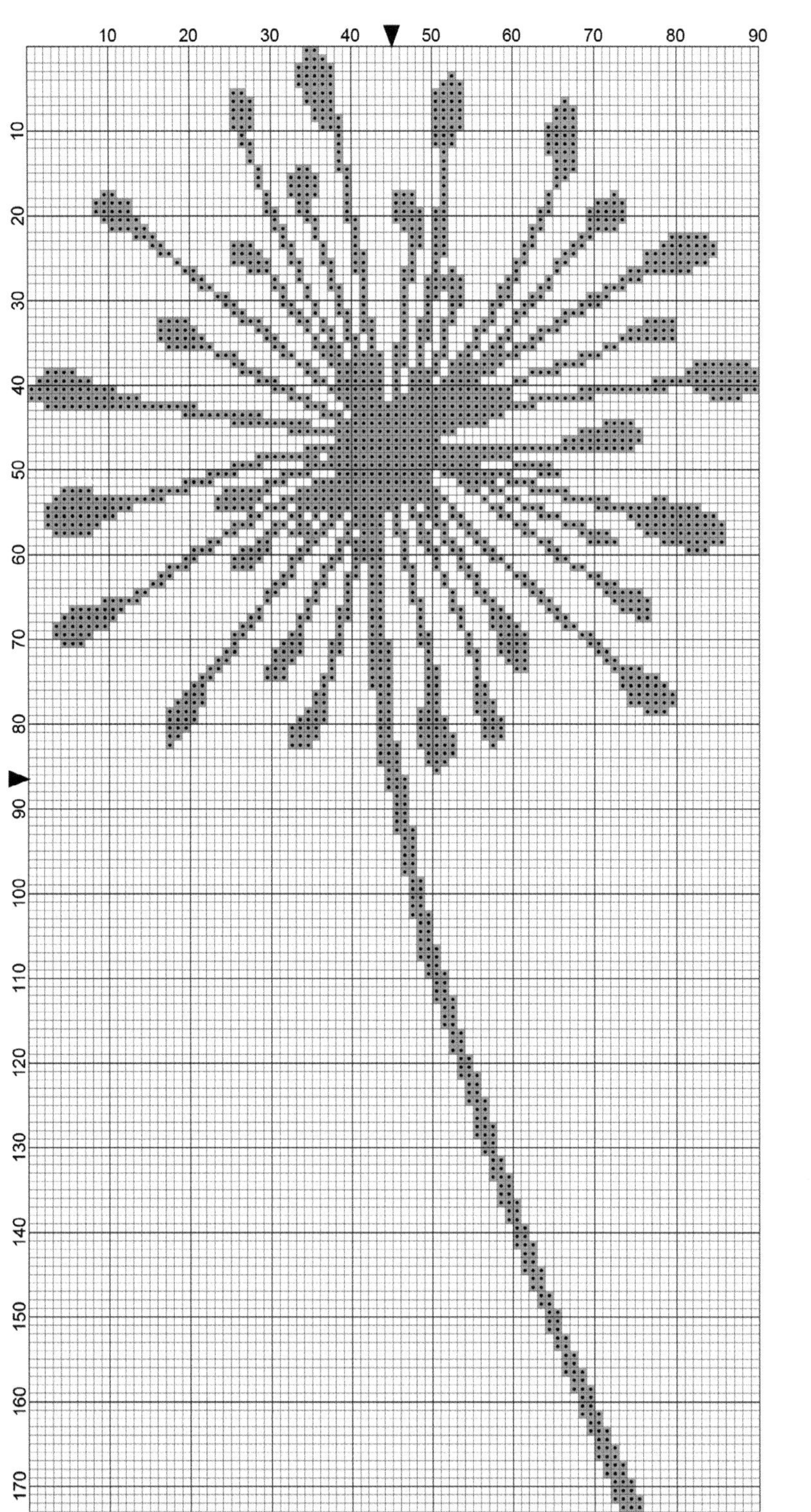

Legend:

DMC-3836

Abstract Dandelion

Thread:
DMC 3836 Grape, Light
(.4 skeins).

Stitch count:
90 × 173.

Design shown:
28-count evenweave over
2 threads, 6⅜" × 12⅜"
(16.2 × 31.4 cm).

Fabric amount:
11" × 17" (28 × 43 cm).

Other fabrics:
16-count over 1 thread: 5⅝" × 10⅞"
(14.3 × 27.6 cm).
Suggested fabric amount: 10" × 15½"
(25.5 × 39.5 cm).

18-count over 1 thread: 5" × 9⅝"
(12.5 × 24.5 cm).
Suggested fabric amount: 9½" × 14"
(24 × 35.5 cm).

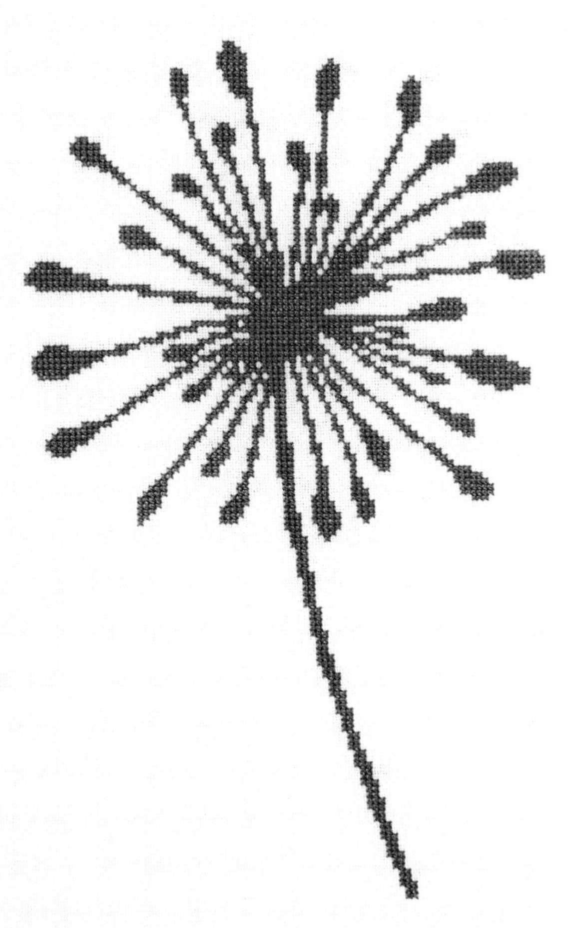

Bonsai

Thread:
DMC 310 Black (.9 skeins).

Stitch count:
214 × 116.

Design shown:
28-count evenweave over 2 threads, 15¼" × 8¼" (38.5 × 21 cm).

Fabric amount:
20" × 13" (51 × 33 cm)

Other fabrics:
16-count over 1 thread: 13⅜" × 8" (34 × 20.5 cm). *Suggested fabric amount:* 18" × 12" (45.5 × 30.5 cm)

18-count over 1 thread: 11⅞" × 6½" (30.2 × 16.5 cm). *Suggested fabric amount:* 16½" × 11" (42 × 28 cm).

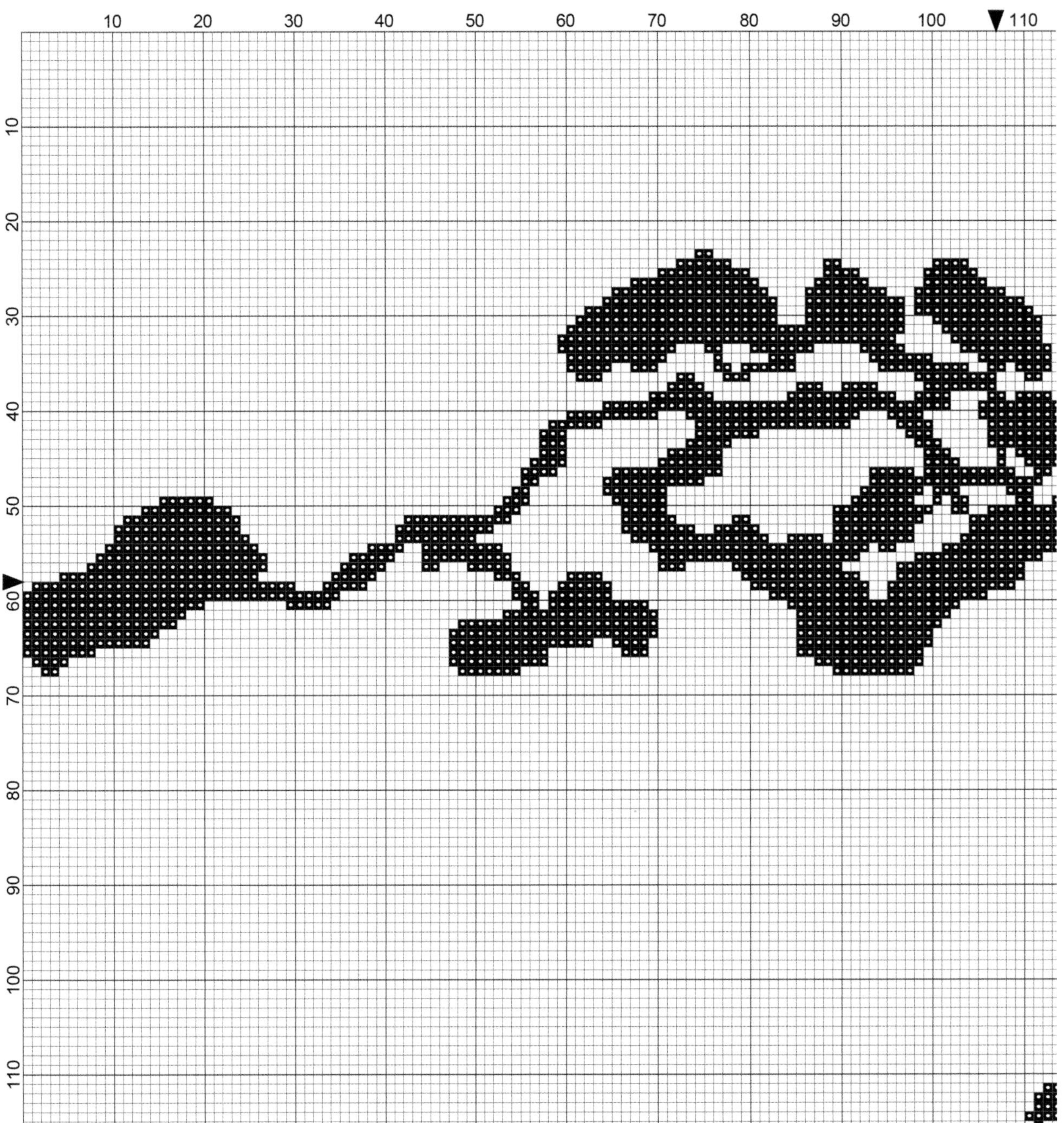

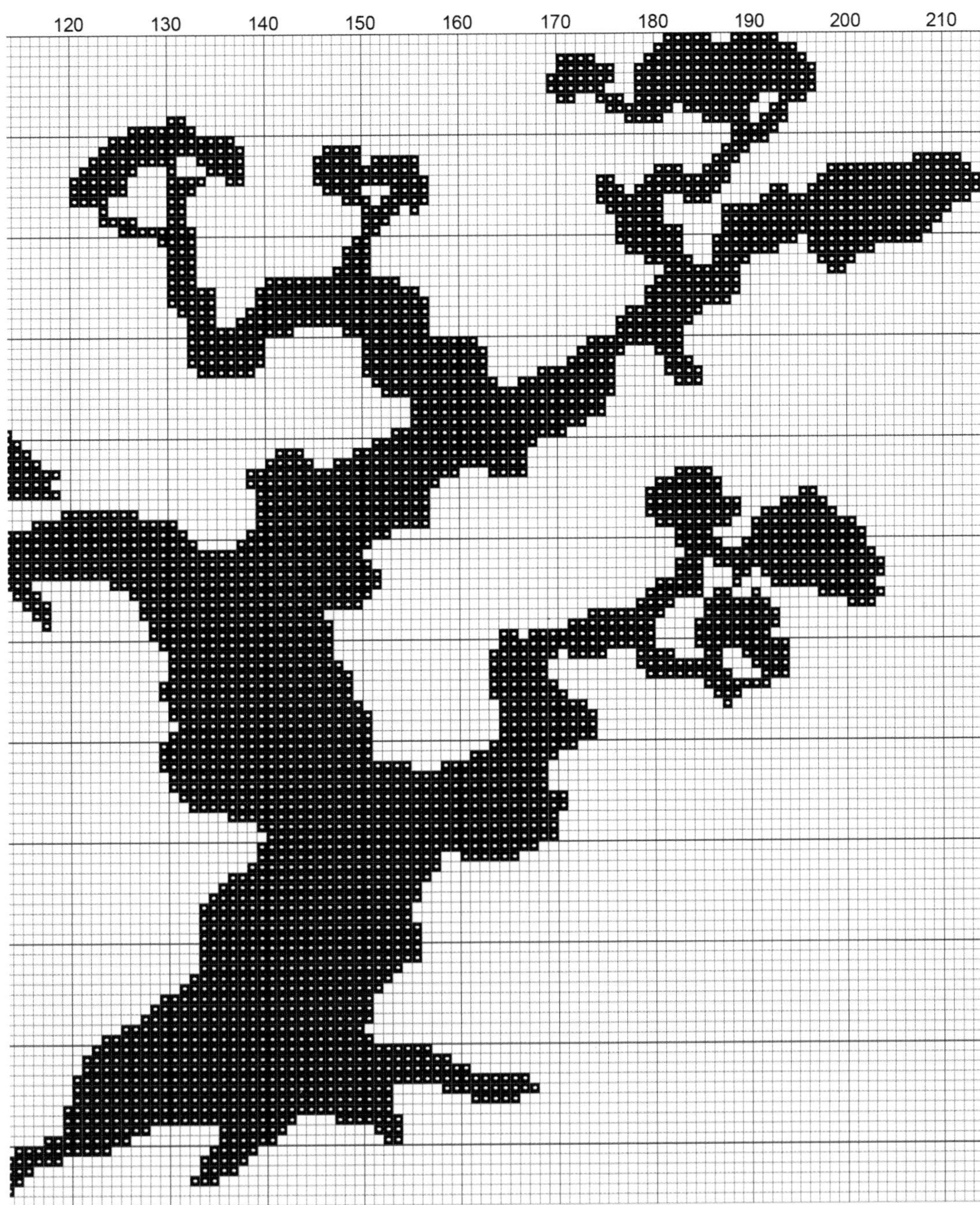

Legend:
DMC-310

Legend:

DMC-White

Cabbage Rose

Thread:
DMC White (1.4 skeins).

Stitch count:
93 × 92.

Design shown:
28-count evenweave over 2 threads, 6⅝" × 6⅝" (16.8 × 16.8 cm).

Fabric amount:
11" × 11" (28 × 28 cm).

Other fabrics:
16-count over 1 thread: 5⅞" × 5⅞" (14.9 × 14.9 cm). *Suggested fabric amount:* 10½" × 10½" (26.5 × 26.5 cm).

18-count over 1 thread: 5⅛" × 5⅛" (13 × 13 cm). *Suggested fabric amount:* 9½" × 9½" (24 × 24 cm).

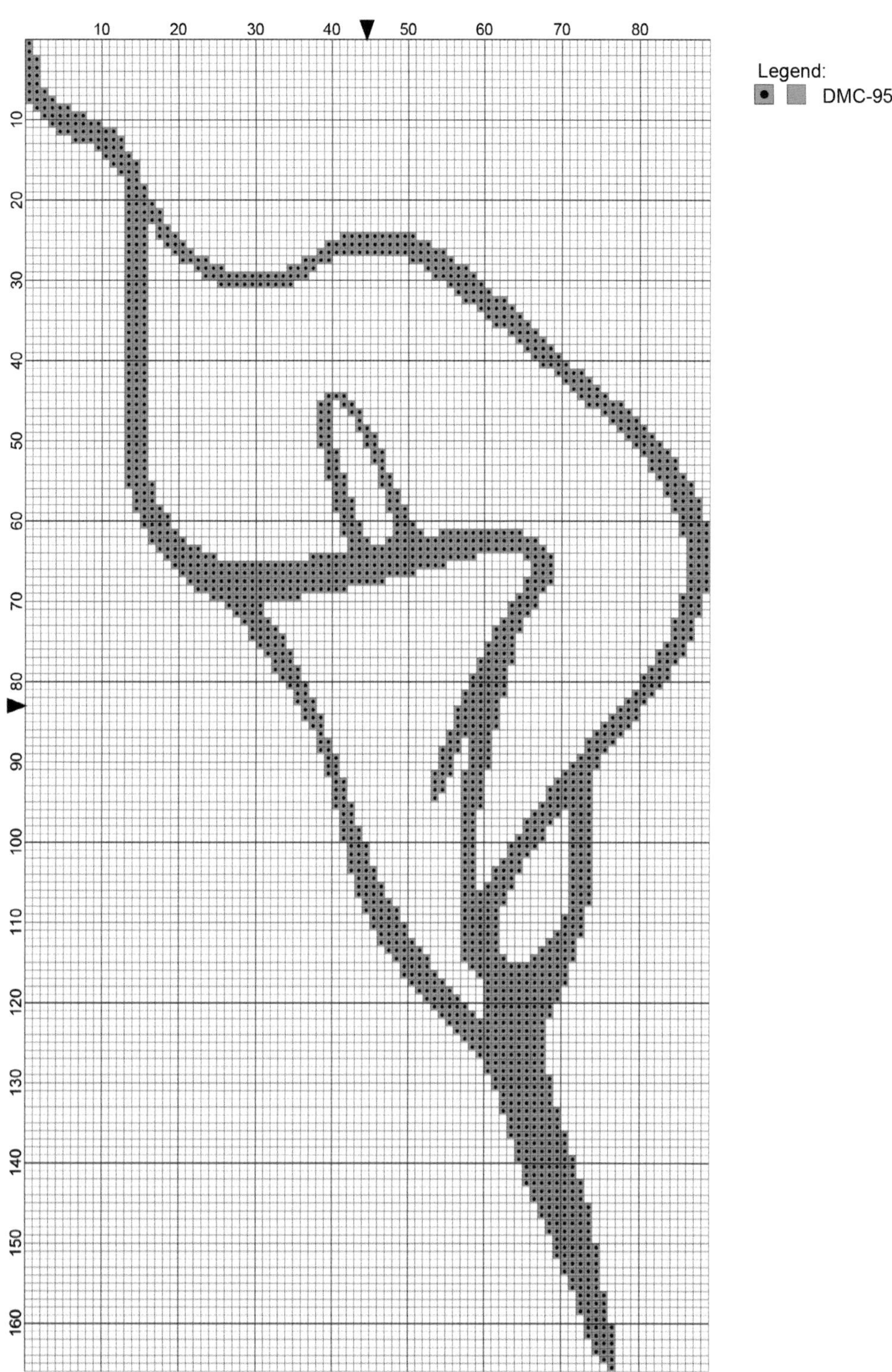

Legend:

DMC-956

Calla Lily

Thread:
DMC 956 Geranium (.3 skeins).

Stitch count:
89 × 166.

Design shown:
28-count evenweave over 2 threads, 6⅜" × 11⅞" (16.2 × 30.2 cm).

Fabric amount:
11" × 16½" (28 × 42 cm).

Other fabrics:
16-count over 1 thread: 5⅝" × 10⅜" (14.3 × 26.3 cm).
Suggested fabric amount: 10" × 15" (25.5 × 38 cm).

18-count over 1 thread: 5" × 9¼" (12.5 × 23.5 cm).
Suggested fabric amount: 9½" × 13½" (24 × 34.5 cm).

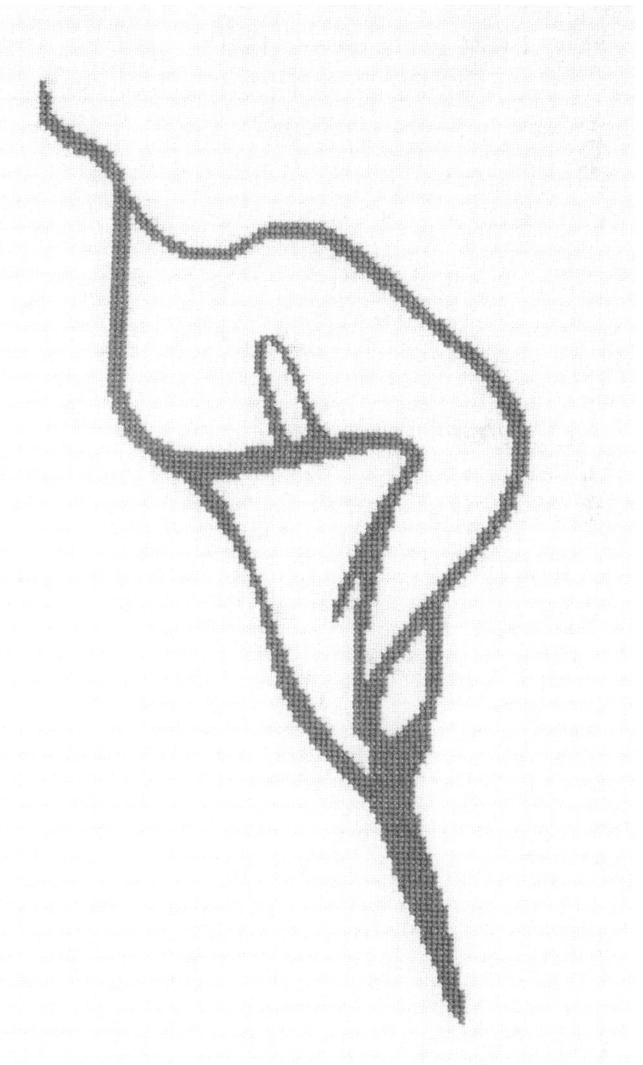

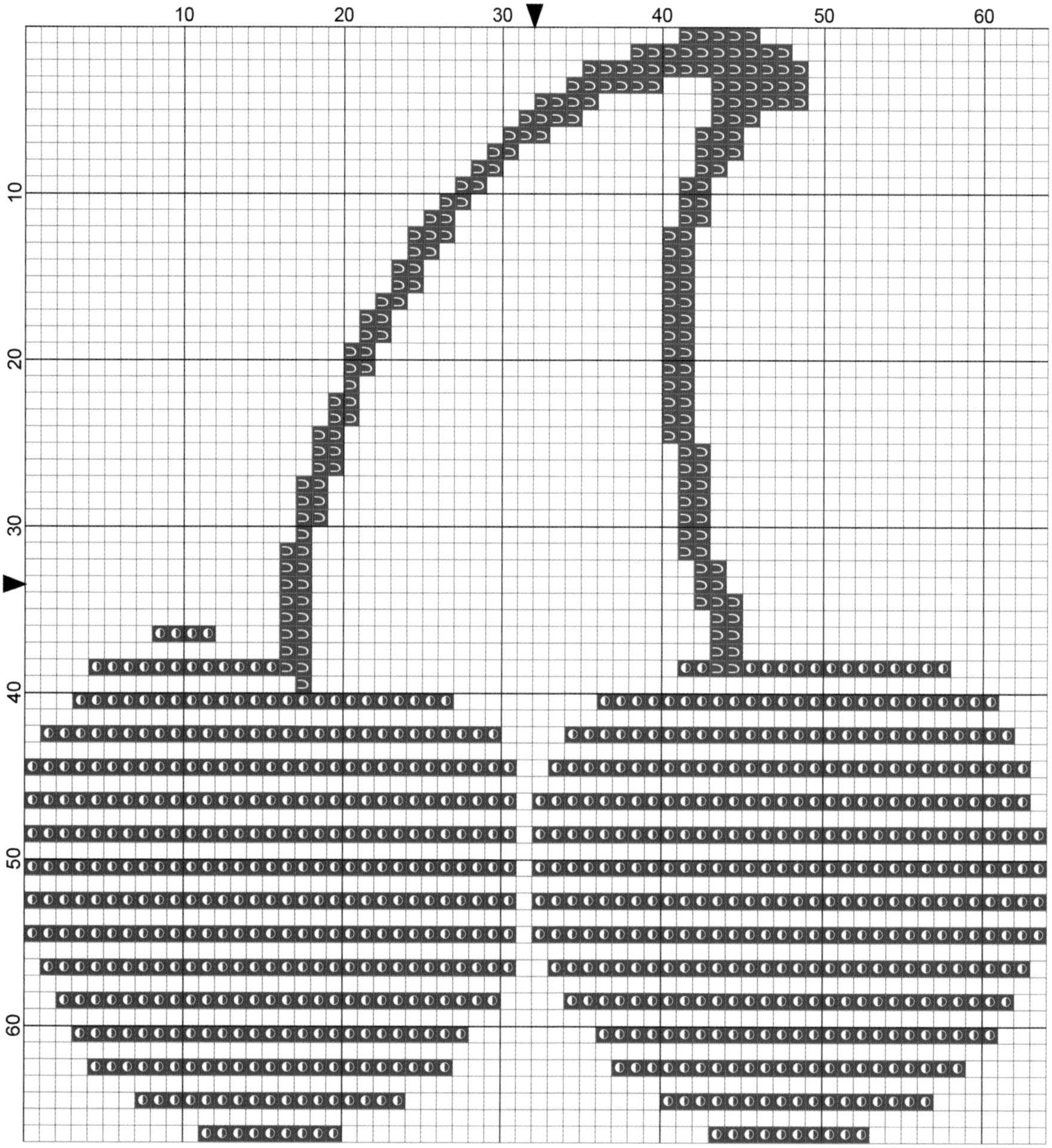

Legend:

DMC-498

DMC-700

Cherries

Thread:
DMC 498 Christmas Red, Dark (.3 skeins).

DMC 335 Rose (.3 skeins).

DMC 367 Pistachio Green, Dark (.2 skeins).

Stitch count:
64 × 67.

Design shown:
28-count evenweave over 2 threads, 4 5/8 "x 4¾" (11.7 × 12 cm).

Fabric amount:
9" × 9½" (23 × 24 cm).

Other fabrics:
16-count over 1 thread: 4" × 4½" (10 × 11.5 cm).
Suggested fabric amount: 8 1/2" × 8½" (21.5 × 21.5 cm).

18-count over 1 thread: 3½" × 3¾" (9 × 9.5 cm).
Suggested fabric amount: 8" × 8" (20.5 × 20.5 cm).

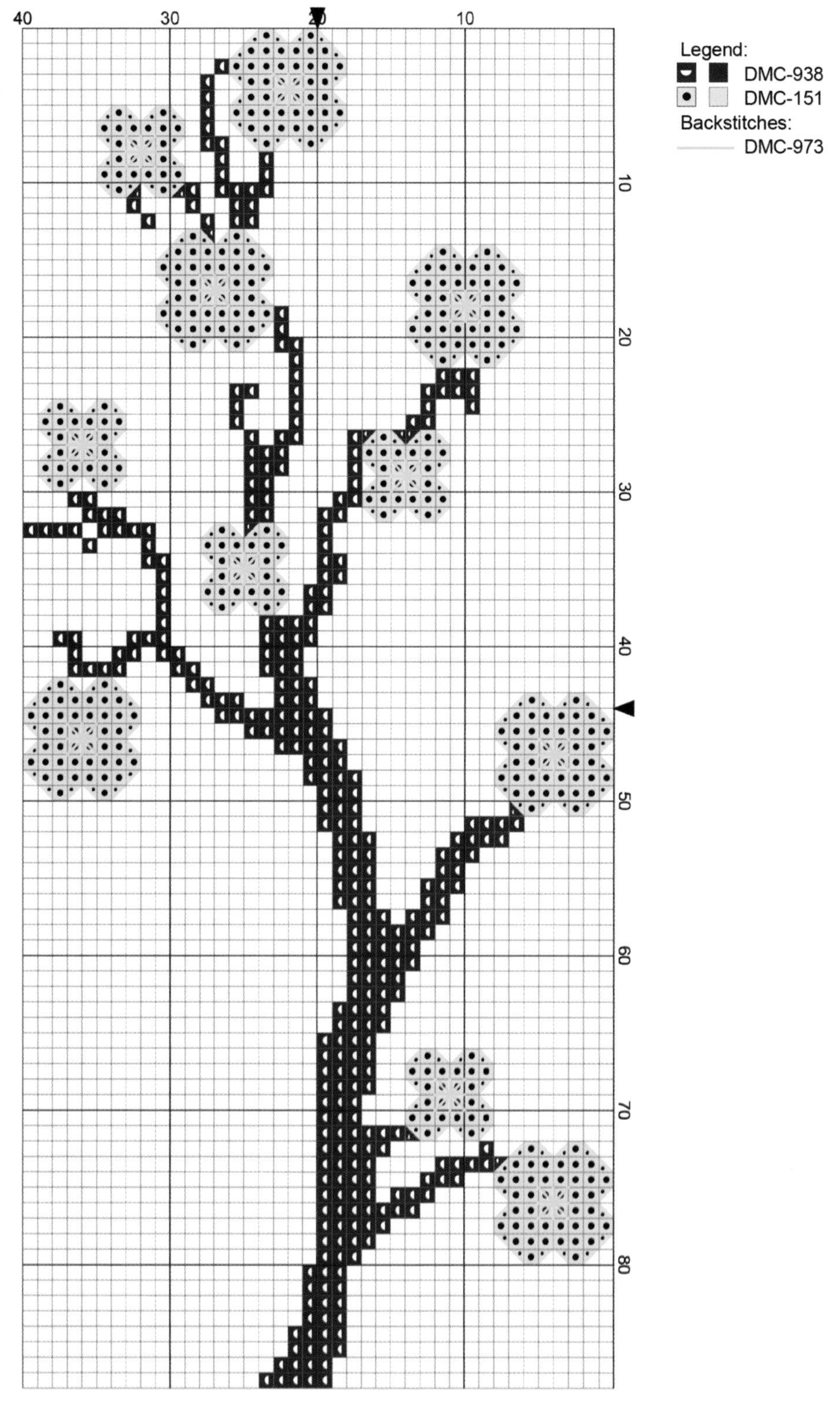

40
30
20
10
10
20
30
40
50
60
70
80
Legend:
DMC-938
DMC-151
Backstitches:
DMC-973

Cherry Blossom

Thread:
DMC 938 Coffee Brown, Ultra Dark (.2 skeins).

DMC 151 Dusty Rose, Ultra Dark (.2 skeins).

DMC 973 Canary, Bright (.1 skeins).

Stitch count:
88 × 40.

Design shown:
28-count evenweave over 2 threads, 6¼" × 2⅞" (16 × 7.3 cm).

Fabric amount:
11" × 7½" (28 × 19 cm).

Other fabrics:
16-count over 1 thread: 5½" × 2½" (14 × 6.5 cm). *Suggested fabric amount:* 10" × 7" (25.5 × 18 cm).

18-count over 1 thread: 4⅞" × 2¼" (12.4 × 5.5 cm). *Suggested fabric amount:* 9½" × 6½" (24 × 16.5 cm).

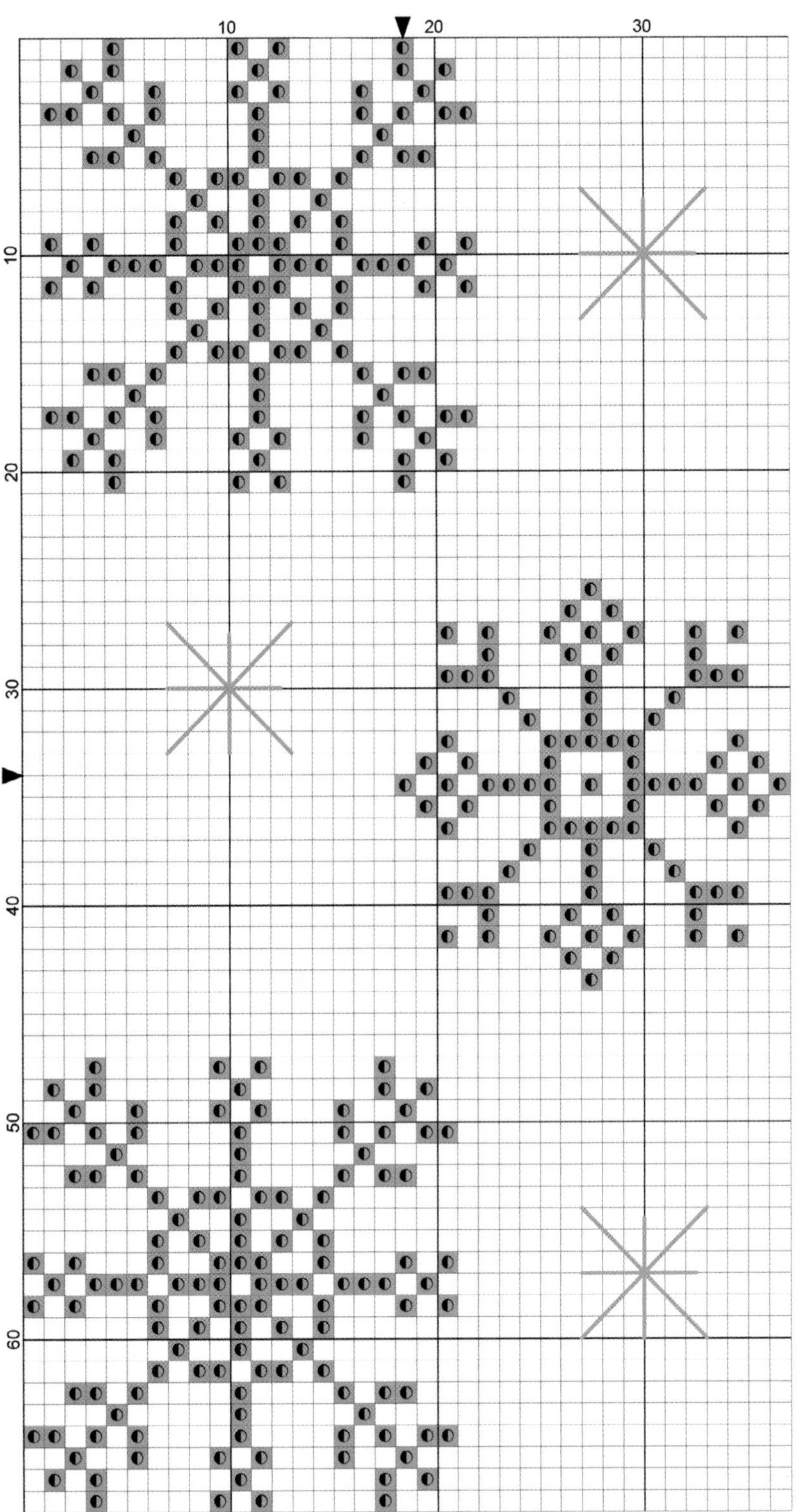

Legend:

DMC-318

Backstitches:

DMC-318

Falling Snowflakes

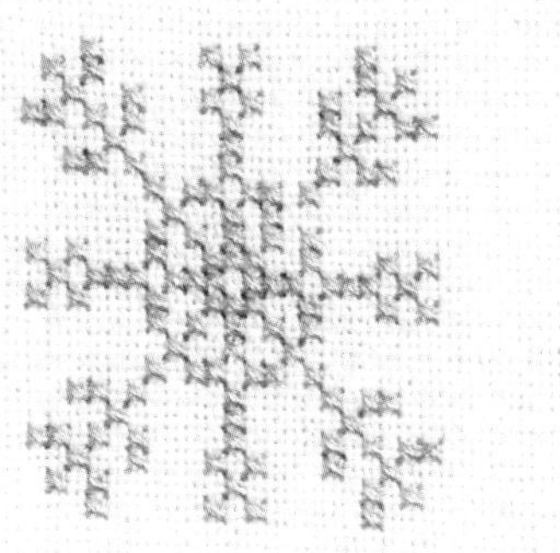

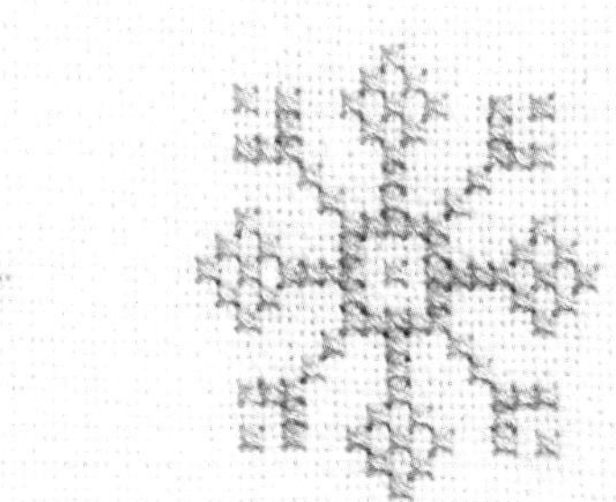

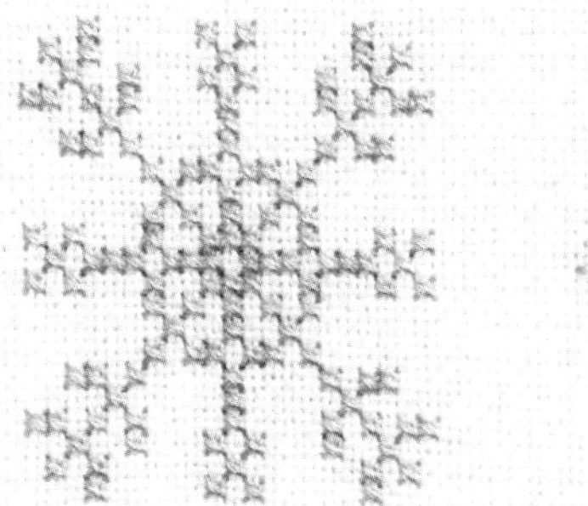

Thread:
DMC 318 Steel Gray, Light (.2 skeins).

Stitch count:
37 × 68.

Design shown:
28-count evenweave over 2 threads, 2⅝" × 4 7/8" (6.7 × 12.4 cm).

Fabric amount:
7" × 9½" (18 × 24 cm).

Other fabrics:
16-count over 1 thread: 2⅜" × 4¼" (6 × 11 cm). *Suggested fabric amount:* 7" × 9" (18 × 23 cm).

18-count over 1 thread: 2" × 3¾" (5 × 9.5 cm). *Suggested fabric amount:* 6½" × 8½" (16.5 × 21.5 cm).

Legend:

DMC-598

Thread:
DMC 598 Turquoise, Light (3.2 skeins).

Stitch count:
108 × 123.

Design shown:
28-count evenweave over 2 threads, 7¾" × 8¾" (19.5 × 22 cm).

Fabric amount:
12" × 13½" (30.5 × 34.5 cm).

Other fabrics:
16-count over 1 thread: 6¾" × 7¾" (17 × 19.5 cm).
Suggested fabric amount: 11" × 12" (28 × 30.5 cm).

18-count over 1 thread: 6" × 6⅞" (15 × 17.5 cm).
Suggested fabric amount: 10½" × 11½" (26.5 × 29 cm).

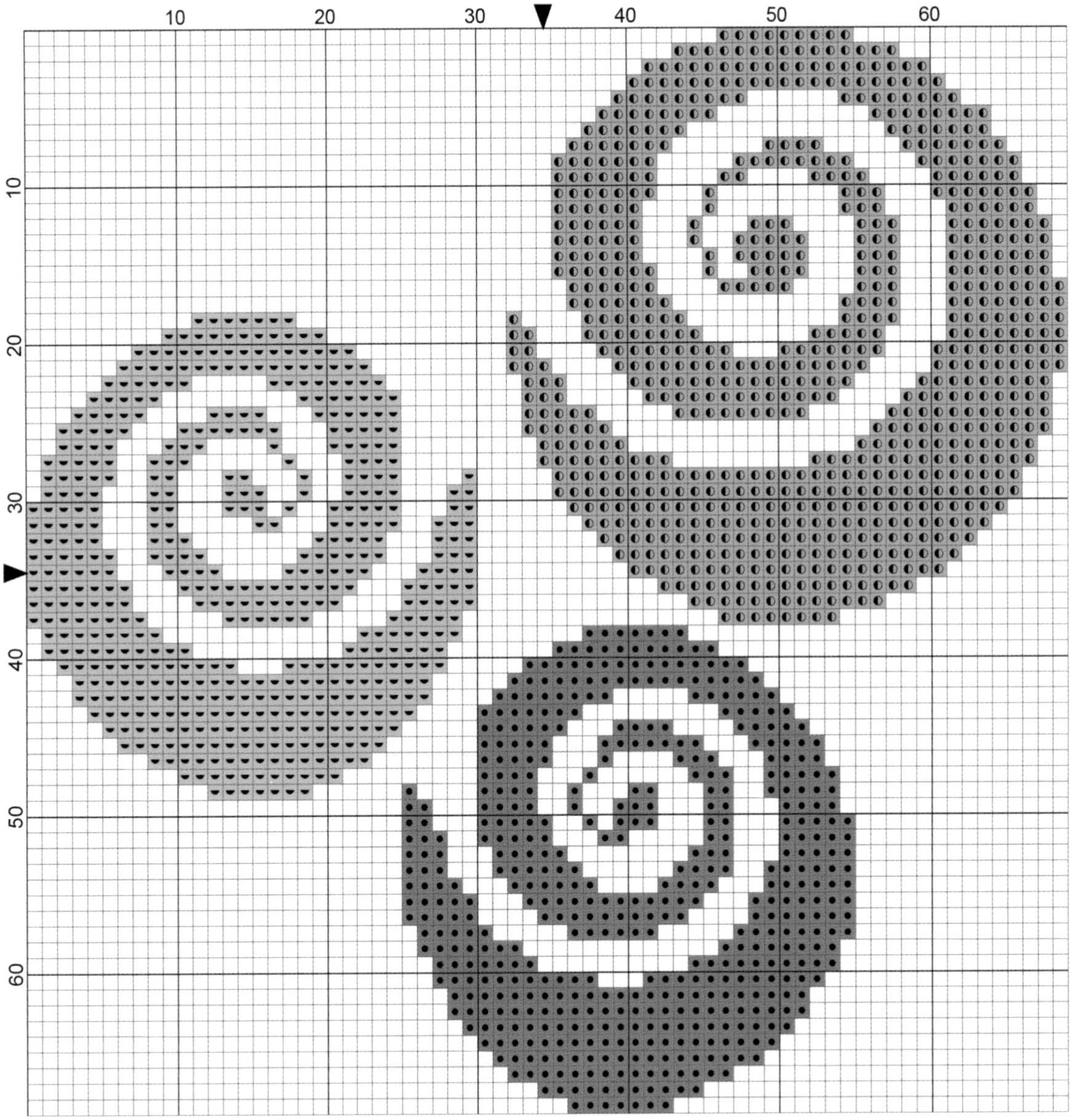

10 20 30 40 50 60

10 20 30 40 50 60

Legend:

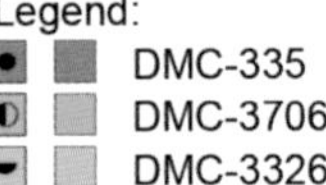

Pink Rosebuds

✖✖✖✖✖✖✖✖✖✖✖

Thread:
DMC 335 Rose (.1 skeins).

DMC 3706 Melon, Medium (.1 skeins).

DMC 3326 Rose, Light (.1 skeins).

Stitch count:
69 × 69.

Design shown:
28-count evenweave over 2 threads, 4⅞" × 4⅞" (12.4 × 12.4 cm).

Fabric amount:
9½" × 9½" (24 × 24 cm).

Other fabrics:
16-count over 1 thread:
4⅜" × 4⅜" (11.1 × 11.1 cm).
Suggested fabric amount:
9" × 9" (23 × 23 cm).

18-count over 1 thread:
3⅞ × 3⅞" (9.8 × 9.8 cm).
Suggested fabric amount:
8½" × 8½" (21.5 × 21.5 cm).

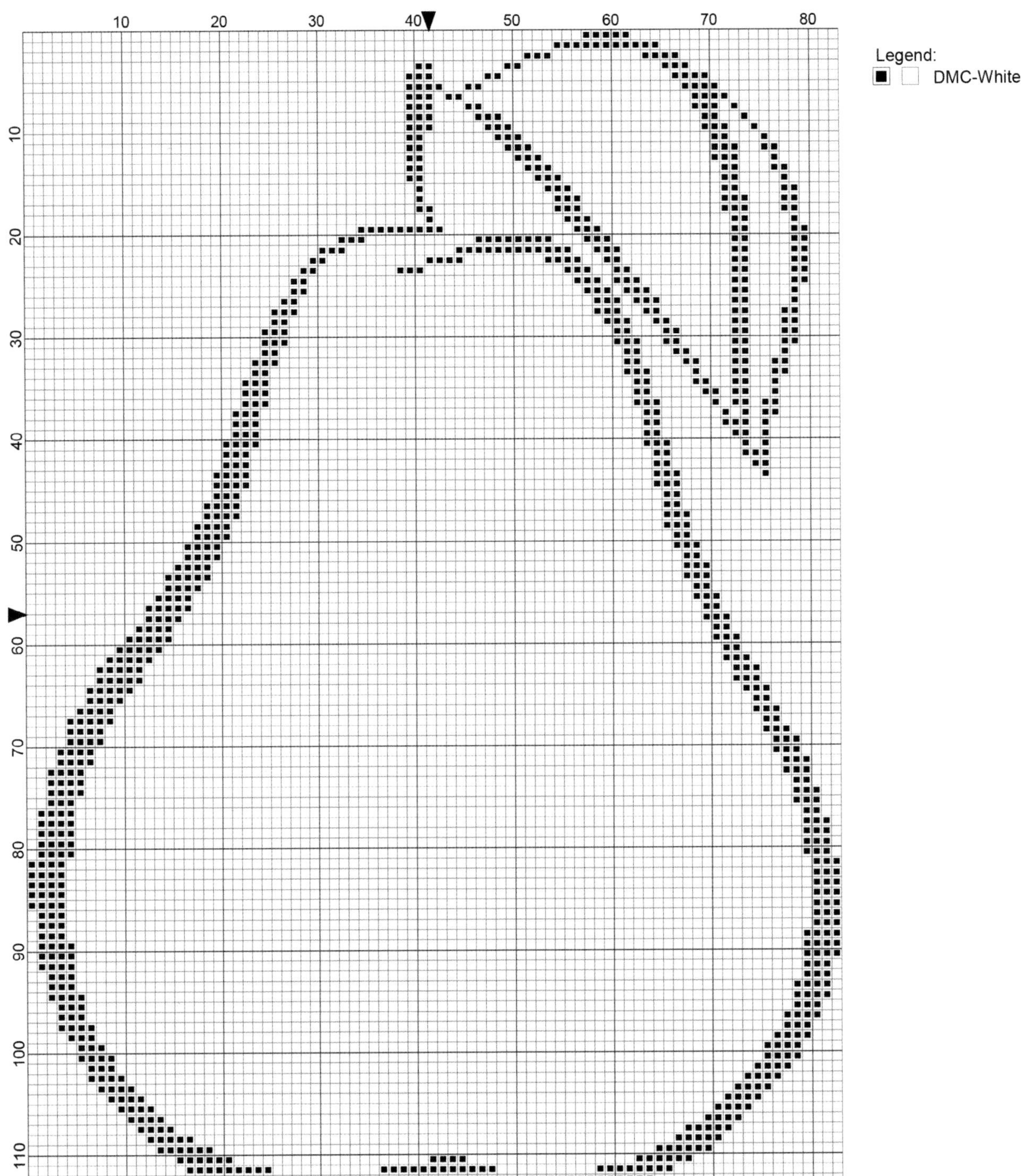

Legend:
■ □ DMC-White

Simple Pear

Thread:
DMC White (.4 skeins).

Stitch count:
83 × 114.

Design shown:
28-count evenweave over 2 threads, 5⅞" × 8⅛" (14.9 × 20.6 cm).

Fabric amount:
10½" × 12½" (26.5 × 31.5 cm).

Other fabrics:
16-count over 1 thread: 5¼" × 7½" (13.5 × 19 cm). *Suggested fabric amount:* 9½" × 11½" (24 × 29 cm).

18-count over 1 thread: 4⅝" × 6⅜" (11.7 × 16.2 cm). *Suggested fabric amount:* 9" × 11" (23 × 28 cm).

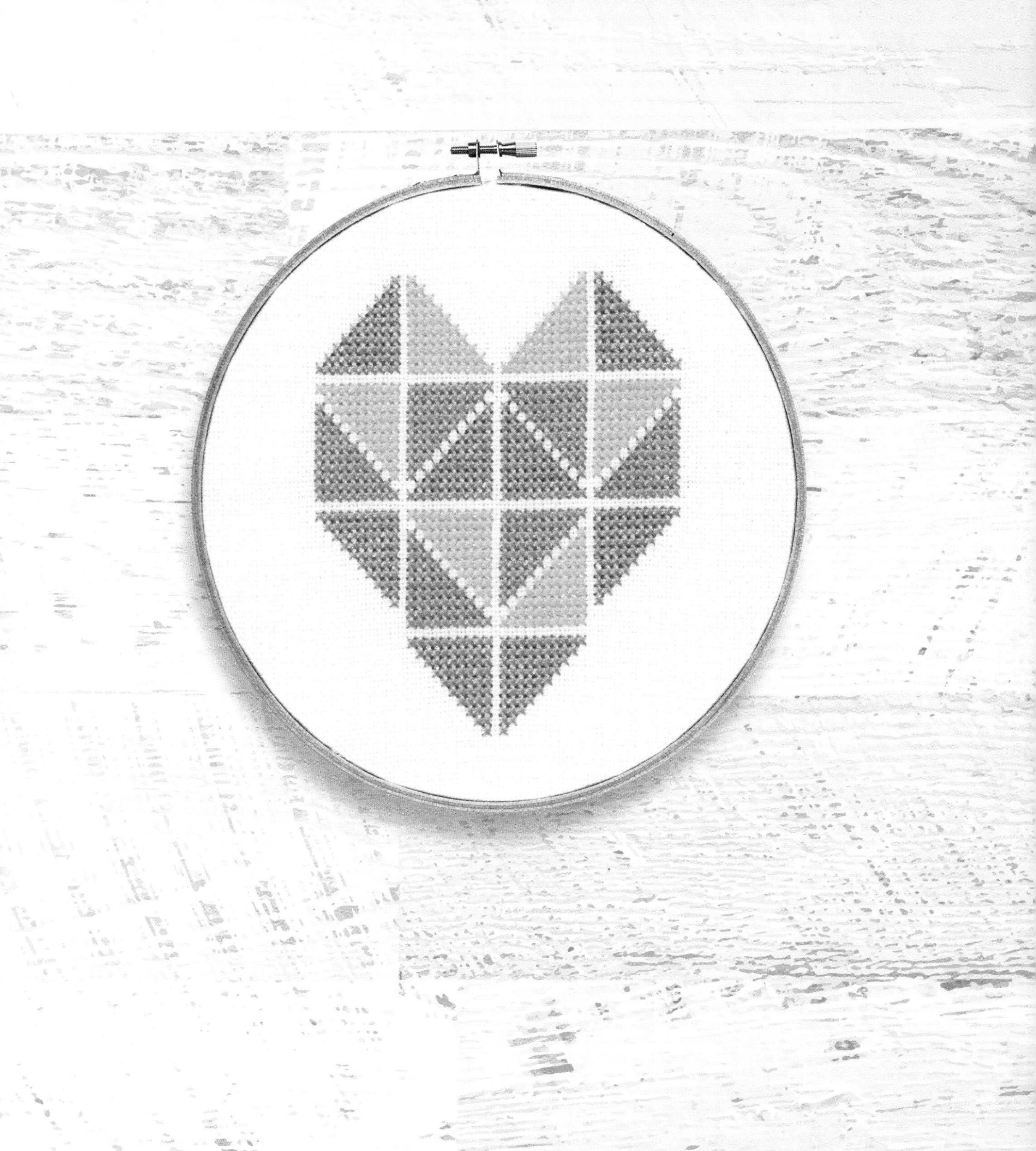

SYMBOLS

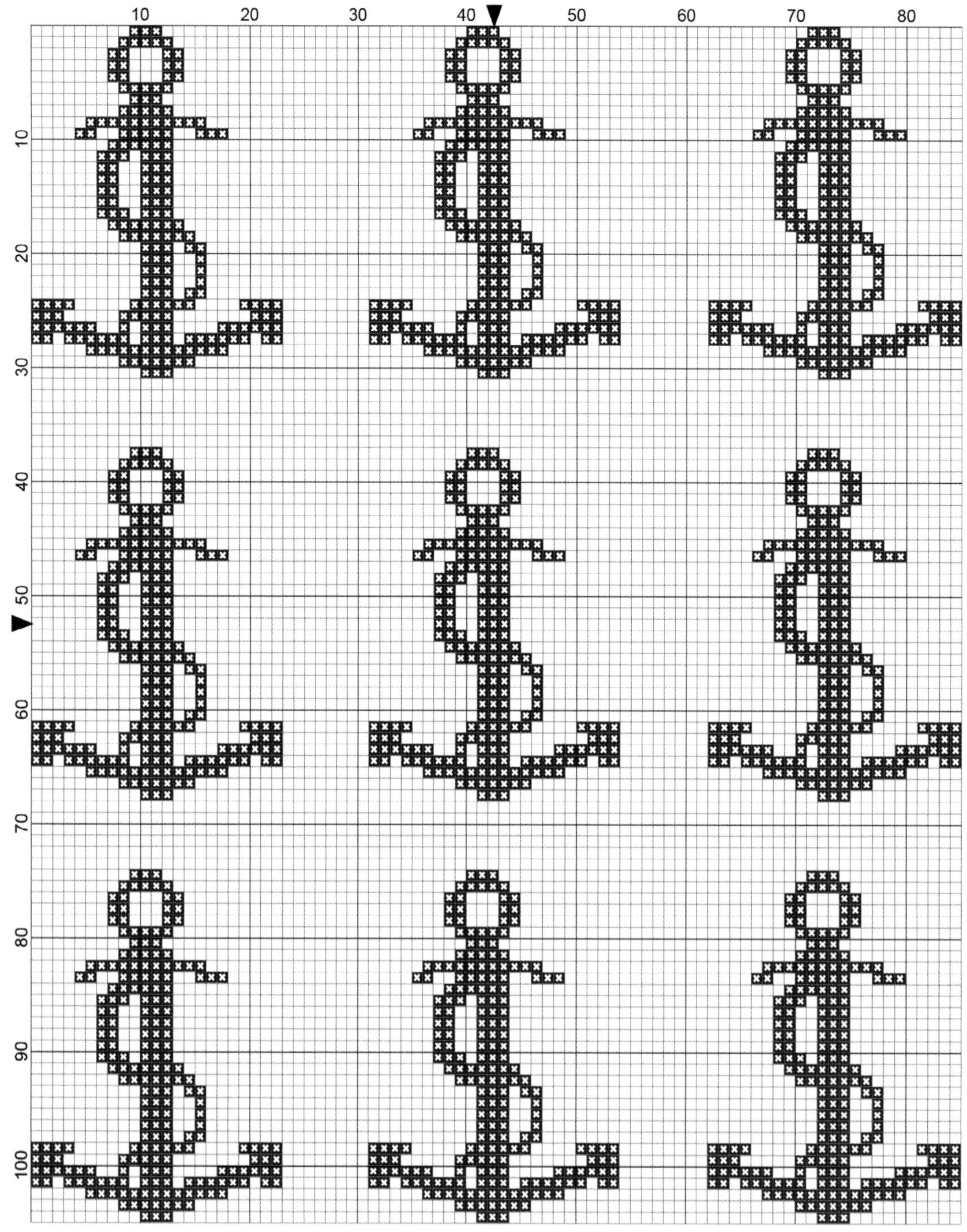

Legend:

DMC-820

Anchors Aweigh

Thread:
DMC 820 Royal Blue, Very Dark (.8 skeins).

Stitch count:
85 × 105.

Design shown:
28-count evenweave over 2 threads, 6⅛" × 7½" (15.5 × 19 cm).

Fabric amount:
10½" × 12" (26.5 × 30.5 cm).

Other fabrics:
16-count over 1 thread: 5⅜" × 6⅝" (13.7 × 16.8 cm). *Suggested fabric amount:* 10" × 11" (25.5 × 28 cm).

18-count over 1 thread: 4¾" × 5⅞" (12 × 14.9 cm). *Suggested fabric amount:* 9" × 10½" (23 × 26.5 cm).

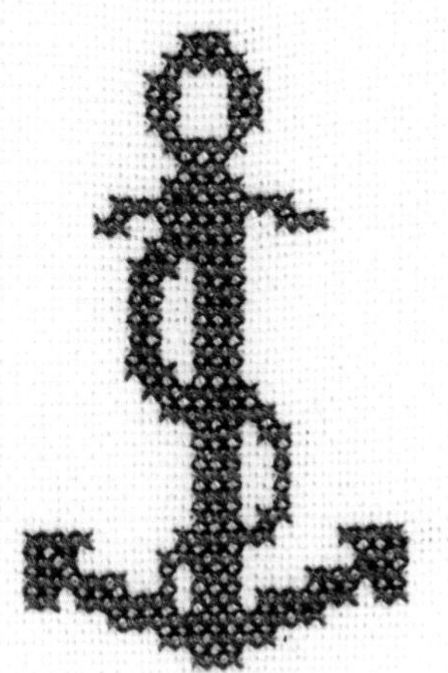

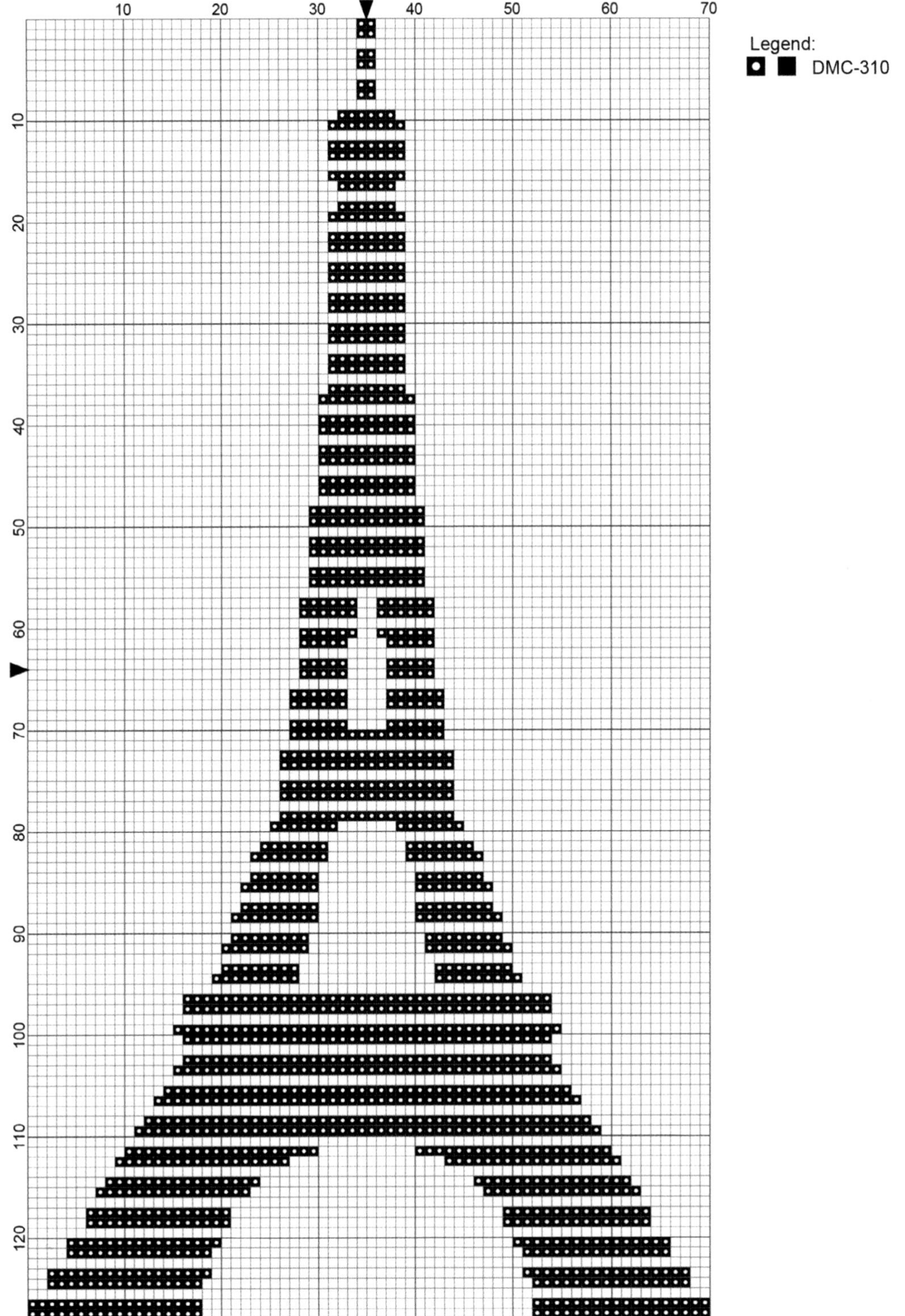

10
20
30
40
50
60
70
Legend:
DMC-310

Eiffel Tower

Thread:
DMC 310 Black (.6 skeins).

Stitch count:
70 × 128.

Design shown:
28-count evenweave over 2 threads, 5" × 9⅛" (12.5 × 23.2 cm).

Fabric amount:
9½" × 13½" (24 × 34.5 cm).

Other fabrics:
16-count over 1 thread: 4⅜" × 8" (11.1 × 20.5 cm). *Suggested fabric amount:* 9" × 12½" (23 × 31.5 cm).

18-count over 1 thread: 3⅞" × 7⅛" (9.8 × 18.2 cm). *Suggested fabric amount:* 8½" × 11½" (21.5 × 29 cm).

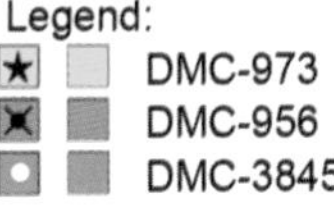
Legend:
DMC-973
DMC-956
DMC-3845

Geometric Heart

✖✖✖✖✖✖✖✖✖✖✖

Thread:
DMC 973 Canary, Bright (.1 skeins).

DMC 956 Geranium (.1 skeins).

DMC 3845 Bright Turquoise, Medium (.2 skeins).

Stitch count:
43 × 47.

Design shown:
28-count evenweave over 2 threads, 3⅛" × 3⅜" (8 × 8.6 cm).

Fabric amount:
8" × 10" (20.5 × 25.5 cm).

Other fabrics:
16-count over 1 thread:
2¾" × 3" (7 × 7.5 cm).
Suggested fabric amount:
7" × 7½" (18 × 19 cm).

18-count over 1 thread:
2⅜" × 2⅝" (6 × 6.7 cm).
Suggested fabric amount:
7" × 7" (18 × 18 cm).

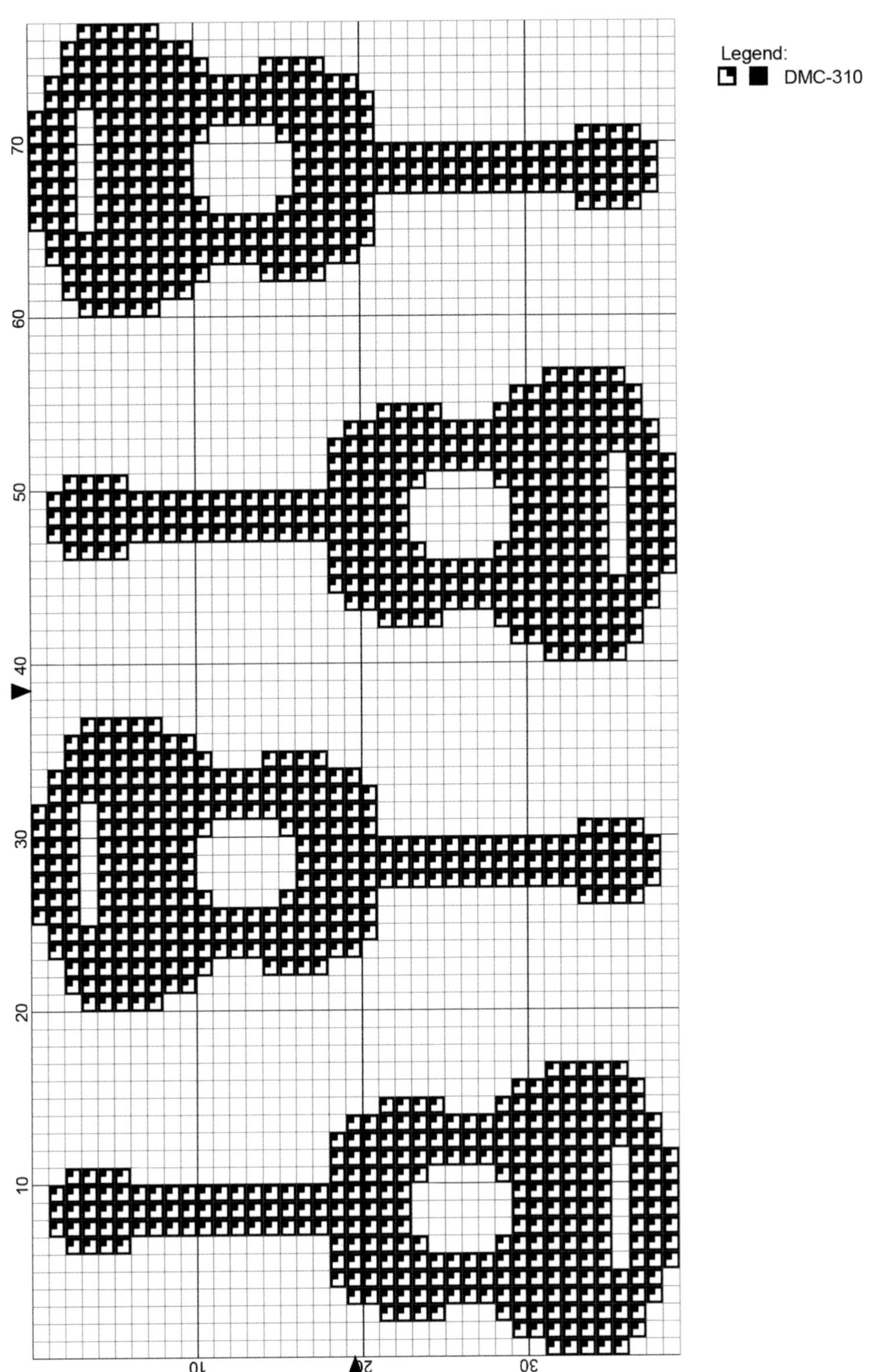
Legend:
DMC-310

Guitars

Thread:
DMC 310 Black (.5 skeins).

Stitch count:
77 × 39.

Design shown:
28-count evenweave over 2 threads, 5½" × 2¾" (14 × 7 cm).

Fabric amount:
10" × 7½" (25.5 × 19 cm).

Other fabrics:
16-count over 1 thread: 4⅞" × 2½" (12.4 × 6.5 cm).
Suggested fabric amount: 9½" × 7" (24 × 18 cm).

18-count over 1 thread: 4¼" × 2⅛" (11 × 5.4 cm).
Suggested fabric amount: 9" × 6½" (23 × 16.5 cm).

Legend:

DMC-209

Hearts in a Heart

Thread:
DMC 209 Lavender, Dark (.4 skeins).

Stitch count:
61 × 61.

Design shown: 28-count evenweave over 2 threads, 4⅜" × 4⅜" (11.1 × 11.1 cm).

Fabric amount:
9" × 9" (23 × 23 cm).

Other fabrics:
16-count over 1 thread:
3⅞" × 3⅞" (9.8 × 9.8 cm).
Suggested fabric amount:
8½" × 8½" (21.5 × 21.5 cm).

18-count over 1 thread:
3⅜" × 3⅜" (8.6 × 8.6 cm).
Suggested fabric amount:
8" × 8" (20.5 × 20.5 cm).

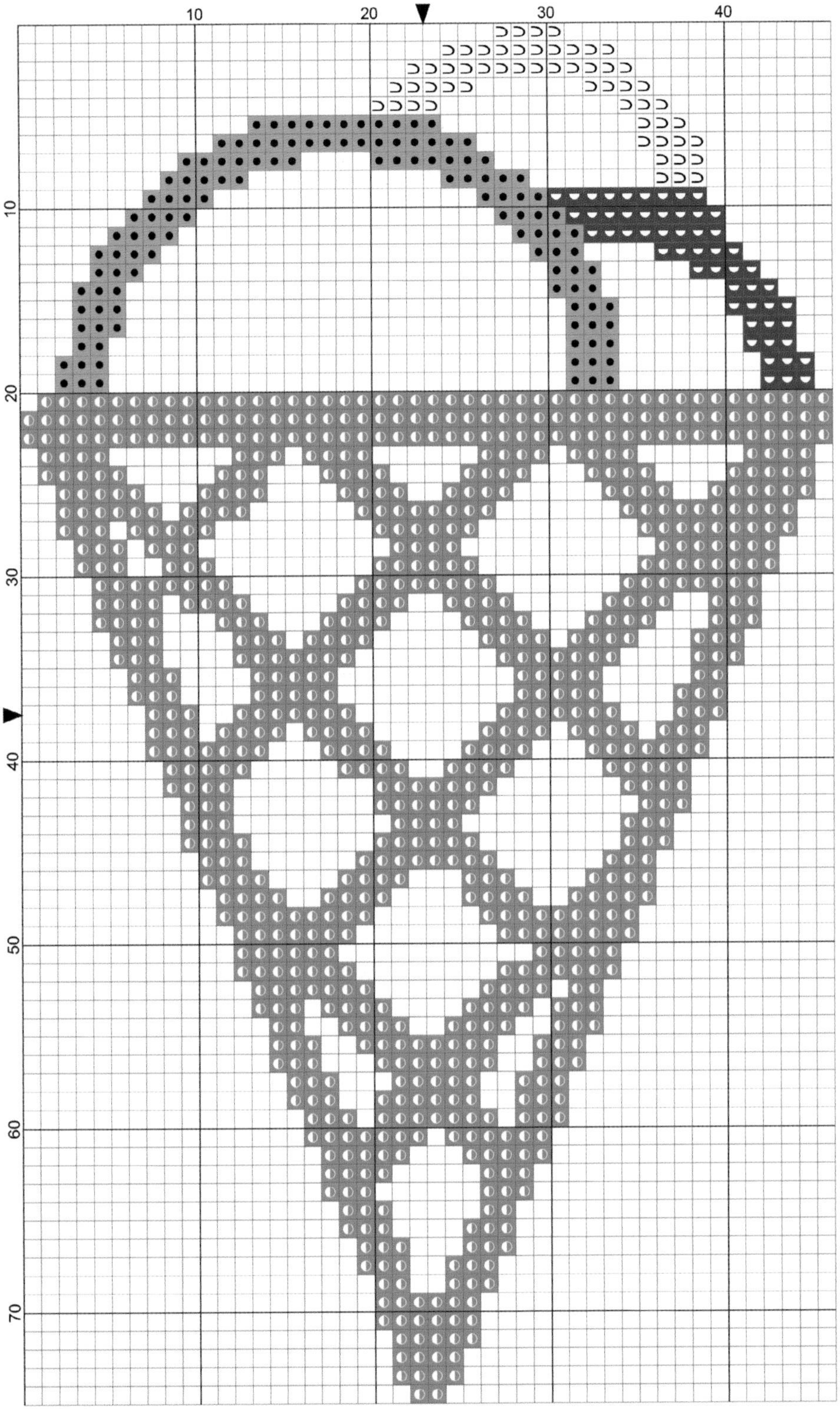

10 20 30 40

10 20 30 40 50 60 70

Legend:

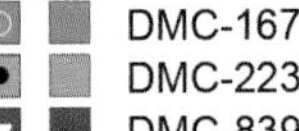

DMC-167

DMC-223

DMC-839

DMC-712

Ice Cream Cone

Thread:
DMC 167 Yellow Beige, Very Dark (.4 skeins).

DMC 223 Shell Pink, Light (.1 skeins).

DMC 839 Beige Brown, Dark, (.1 skeins).

DMC 712 Cream (.1 skeins).

Stitch count:
46 × 75.

Design shown:
28-count evenweave over 2 threads, 3¼" × 5⅜" (8.5 × 13.7 cm).

Fabric amount:
8" × 10" (20.5 × 25.5 cm).

Other fabrics:
16-count over 1 thread: 2⅞" × 4¾" (7.3 × 12 cm). *Suggested fabric amount:* 7½" × 9" (19 × 23 cm).

18-count over 1 thread: 2½" × 4⅛" (6.5 × 10.5 cm). *Suggested fabric amount:* 7" × 8½" (18 × 21.5 cm).

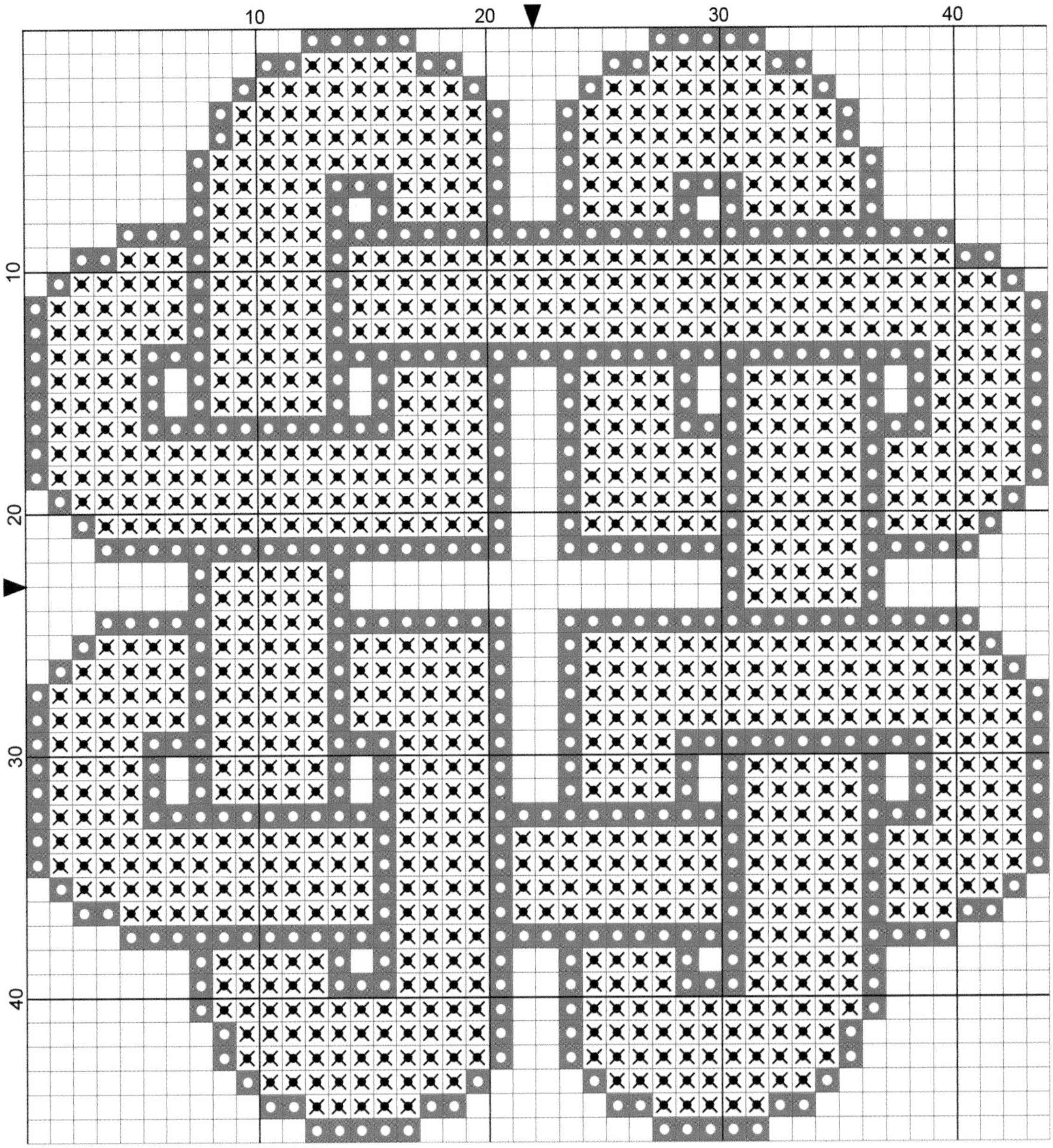

Legend:
DMC-840
DMC-3865

Knotted Hearts

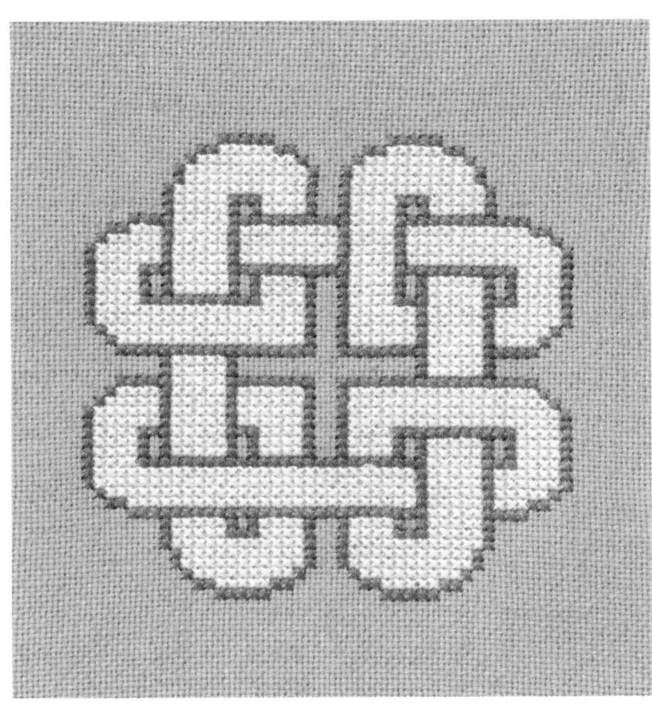

Thread:
DMC 840 Beige Brown, Medium (.2 skeins).

DMC 3865 Winter White (.4 skeins).

Stitch count:
44 × 46.

Design shown:
28-count evenweave over 2 threads, 3⅛" × 3¼" (8 × 8.5 cm).

Fabric amount:
7½" × 8" (19 × 20.5 cm).

Other fabrics:
16-count over 1 thread: 2¾" × 2⅞" (7 × 7.3 cm).
Suggested fabric amount: 7" × 7½" (18 × 19 cm).

18-count over 1 thread: 2½" × 2½" (6.5 × 6.5 cm).
Suggested fabric amount: 7" × 7" (18 × 18 cm).

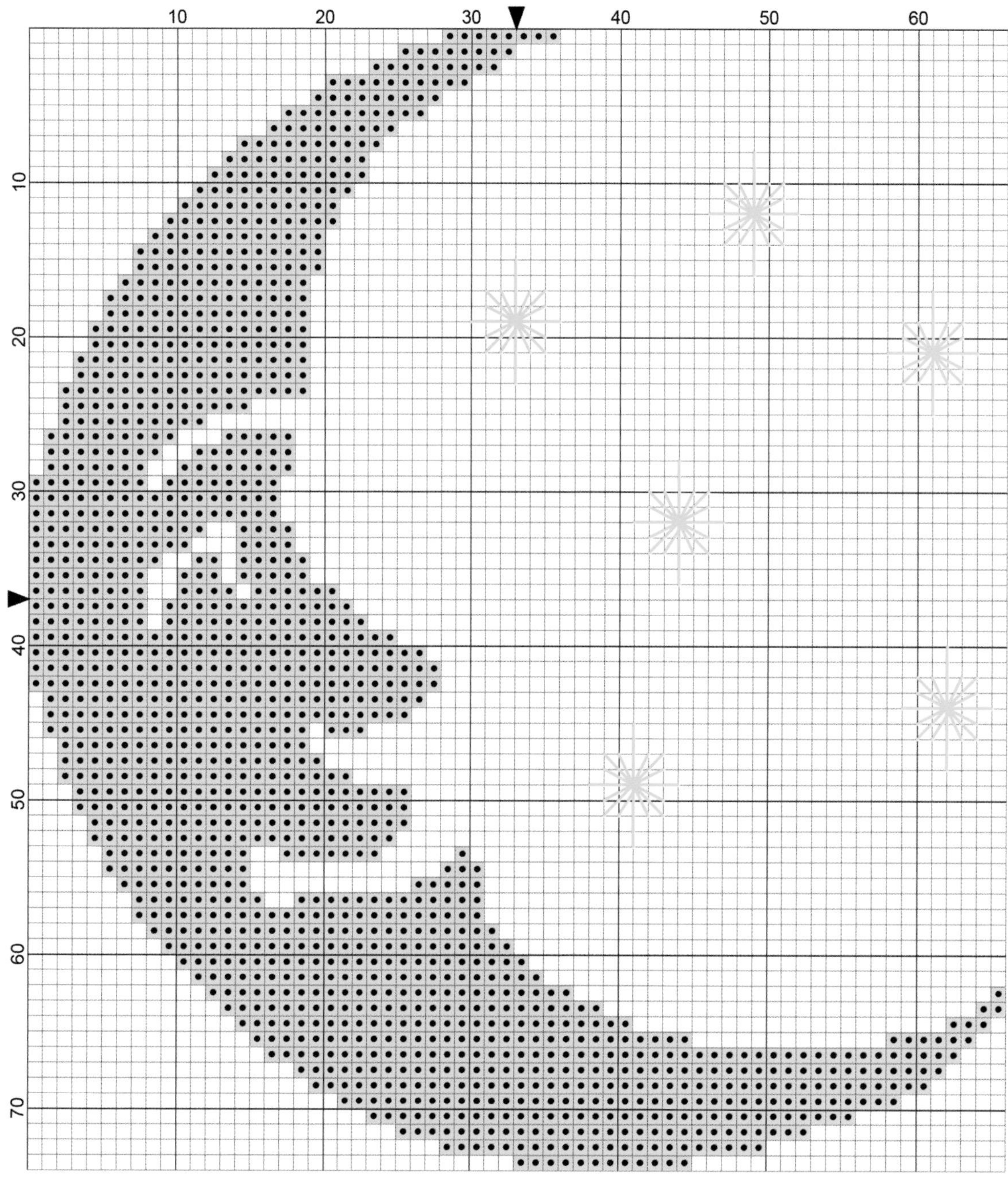

Legend:

DMC-973

Backstitches:

DMC-973

Moon & Stars

Thread:
DMC 973 Canary, Bright (1.2 skeins).

Stitch count:
66 × 74.

Design shown:
28-count evenweave over 2 threads and measures 4¾" × 5¼" (12 × 13.5 cm).

Fabric amount:
9" × 10" (23 × 25.5 cm).

Other fabrics:
16-count over 1 thread:
4⅛" × 4⅝" (10.5 × 11.7 cm).
Suggested fabric amount:
8½" × 9" (21.5 × 23 cm).

18-count over 1 thread:
3⅝" × 4⅛" (9.2 × 10.5 cm).
Suggested fabric amount:
8" × 8½" (20.5 × 21.5 cm).

Legend:
DMC-646

Om

✖✖✖✖✖✖✖✖✖✖✖✖

Thread:
DMC 646 Beaver Gray, Dark (.4 skeins).

Stitch count:
75 × 73.

Design shown:
28-count evenweave over 2 threads, 5⅜" × 5¼" (13.7 × 13.5 cm).

Fabric amount:
10" × 10" (25.5. × 25.5 cm).

Other fabrics:
16-count over 1 thread: 4¾" × 4⅝" (12 × 11.7 cm).
Suggested fabric amount: 9" × 9" (23 × 23 cm)

18-count over 1 thread: 4⅛" × 4" (10.5 × 10 cm).
Suggested fabric amount: 8½" × 8½" (21.5 × 21.5 cm).

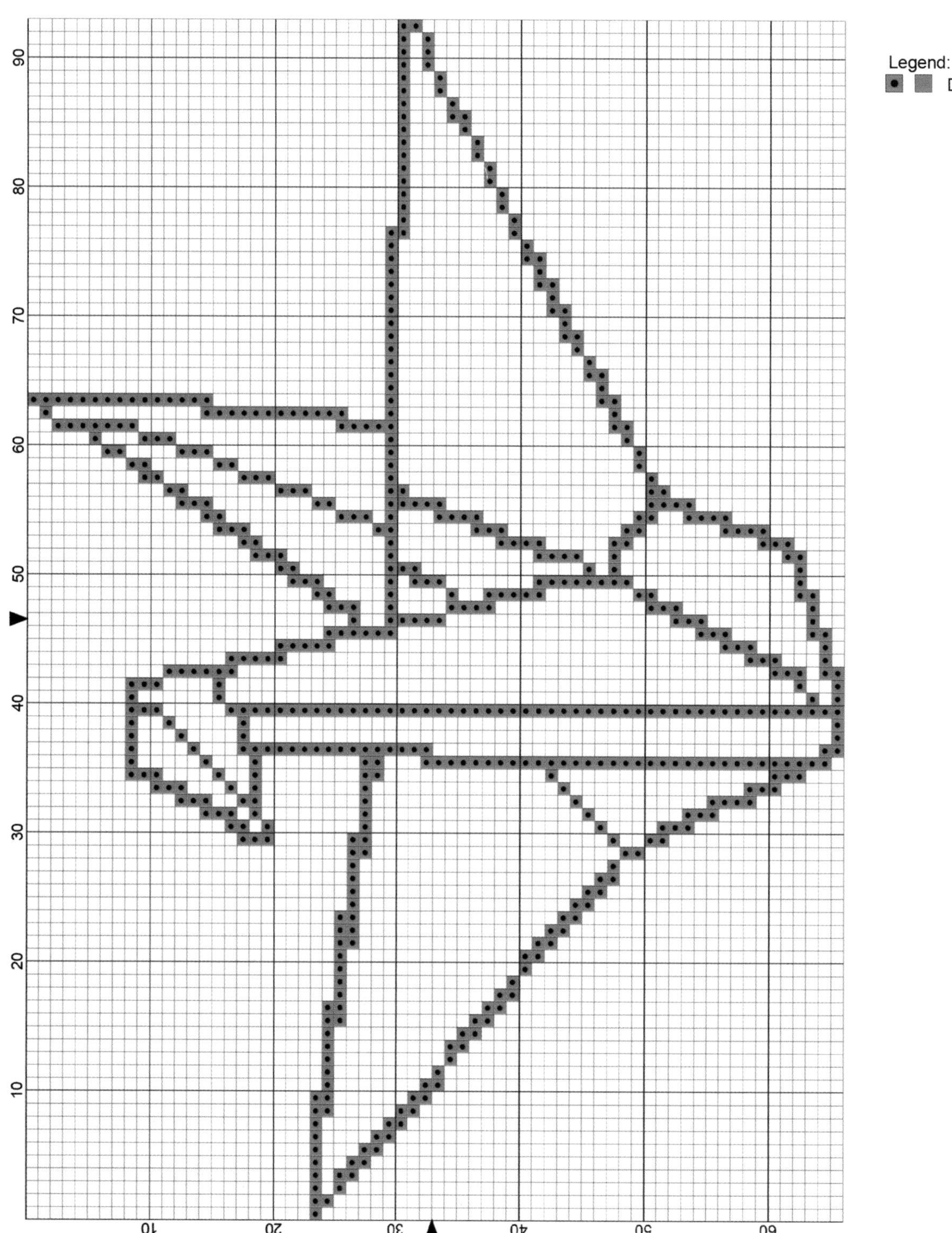
Legend:
DMC-891

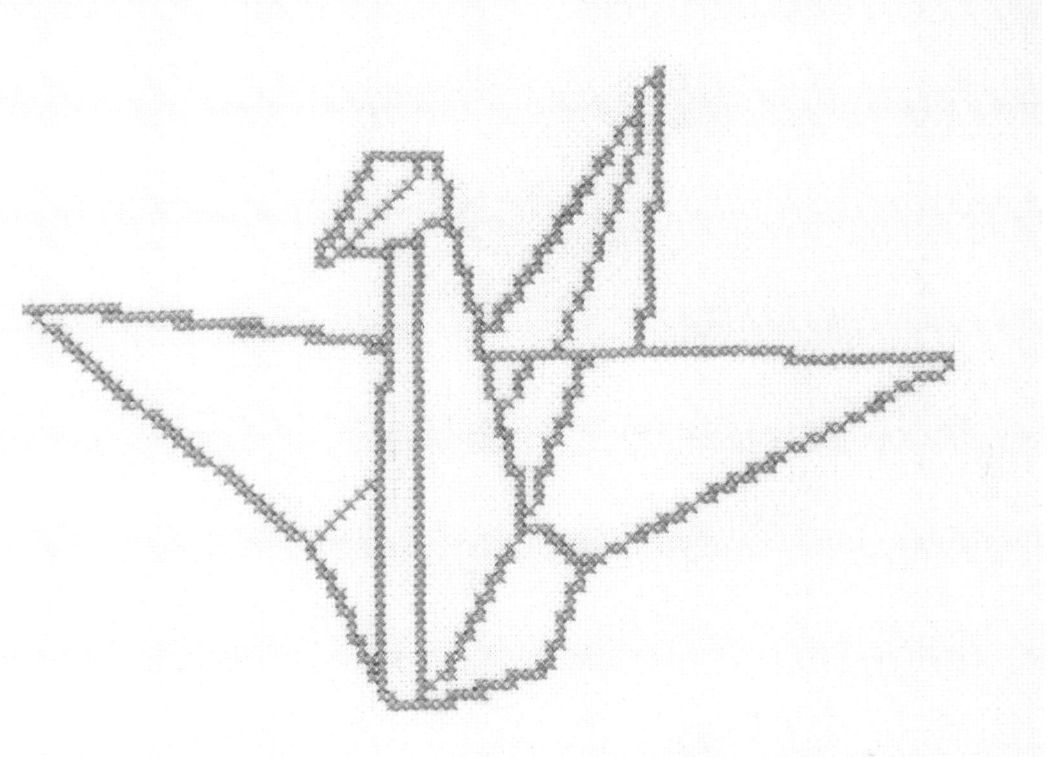

Paper Crane

Thread:
DMC 891 Carnation, Dark (.2 skeins).

Stitch count:
93 × 66.

Design shown:
28-count evenweave over 2 threads, 6⅝" × 4¾" (16.8 × 12 cm).

Fabric amount:
11" × 9" (28 × 23 cm).

Other fabrics:
16-count over 1 thread: 5⅞" × 4⅛" (14.9 × 10.5 cm). *Suggested fabric amount:* 10½" × 8½" (26.5 × 21.5 cm)

18-count over 1 thread: 5⅛" × 3⅝" (13 × 9.2 cm). *Suggested fabric amount:* 9½" × 8" (24 × 20.5 cm).

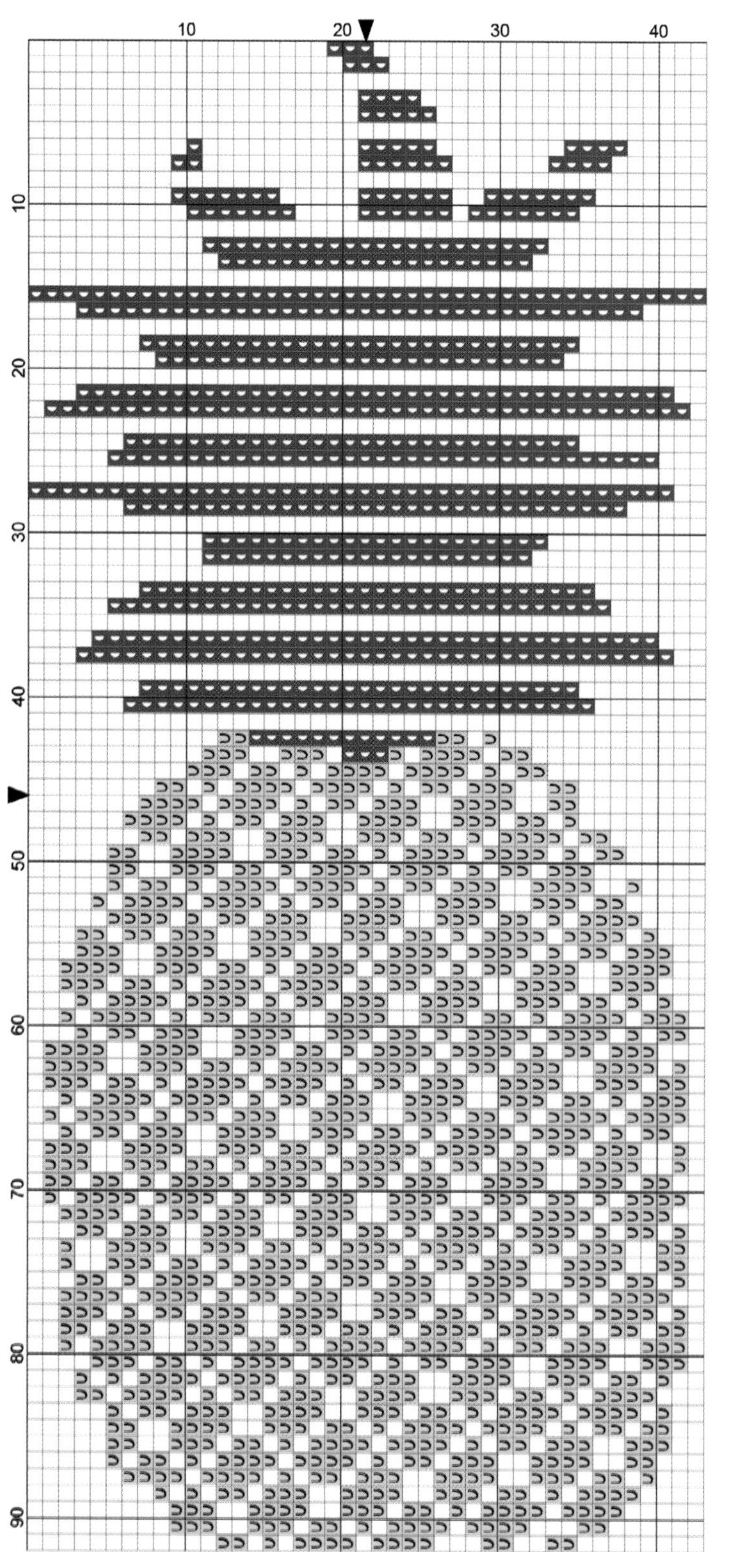

Legend:

DMC-561

DMC-444

Pineapple

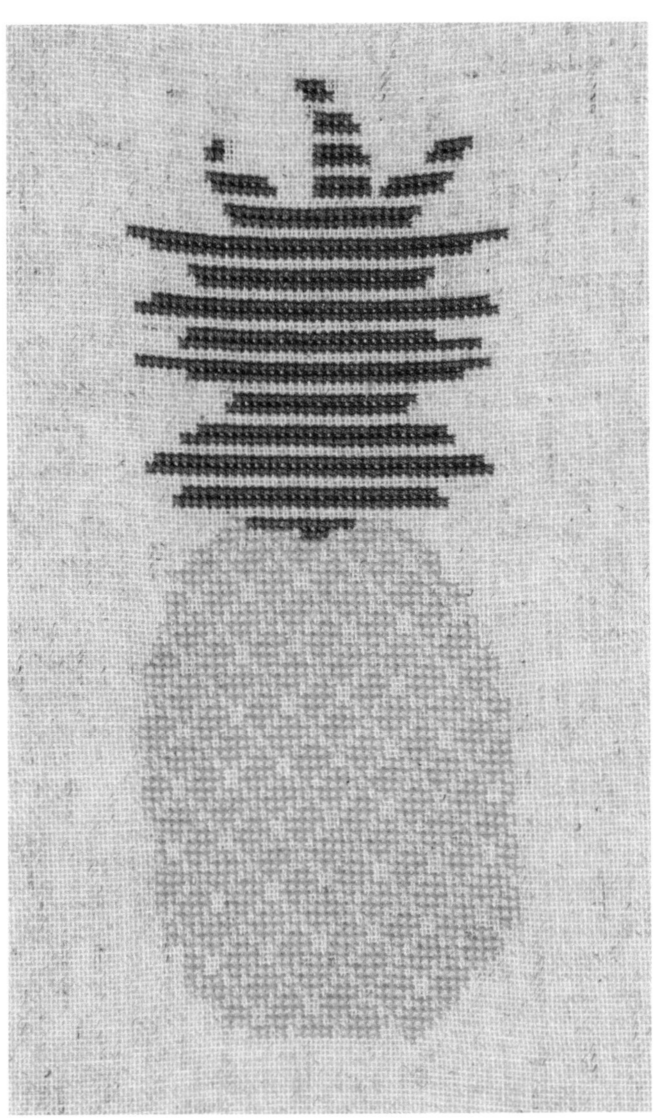

xxxxxxxxxxxx

Thread:
DMC 561 Jade, Very Dark (.3 skeins).

DMC 444 Lemon, Dark (.5 skeins).

Stitch count:
43 × 92.

Design shown:
28-count evenweave over 2 threads, 3⅛" × 6⅝" (8 × 16.8 cm).

Fabric amount:
7½" × 11" (19 × 28 cm).

Other fabrics:
16-count over 1 thread: 2¾" × 5¾" (7 × 14.5 cm).
Suggested fabric amount: 7" × 10" (18 × 25.5 cm).

18-count over 1 thread: 2⅜" × 5⅛" (6 × 13 cm).
Suggested fabric amount: 7" × 9½" (18 × 24 cm).

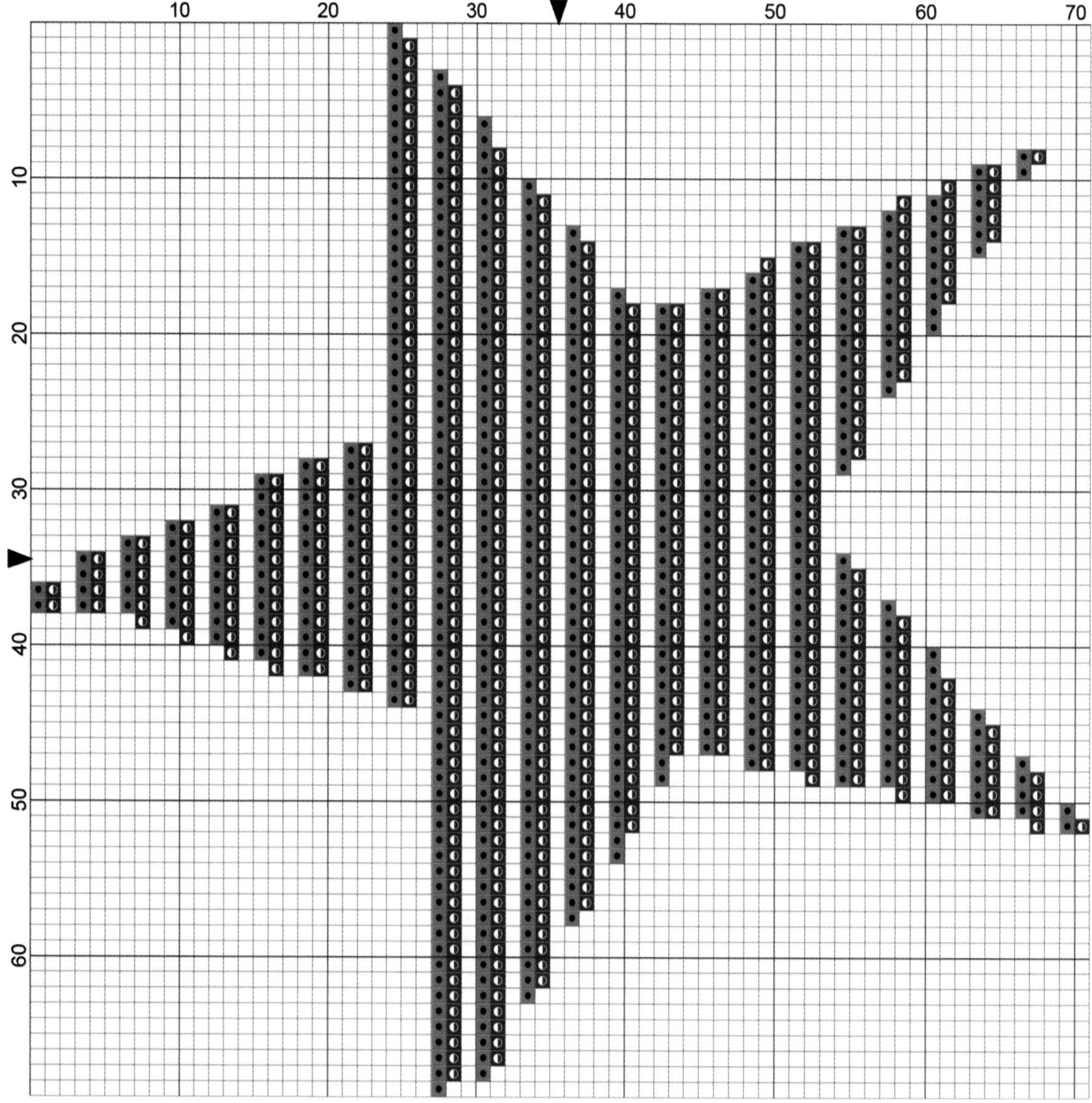

Legend:
DMC-309
DMC-311

Striped Star

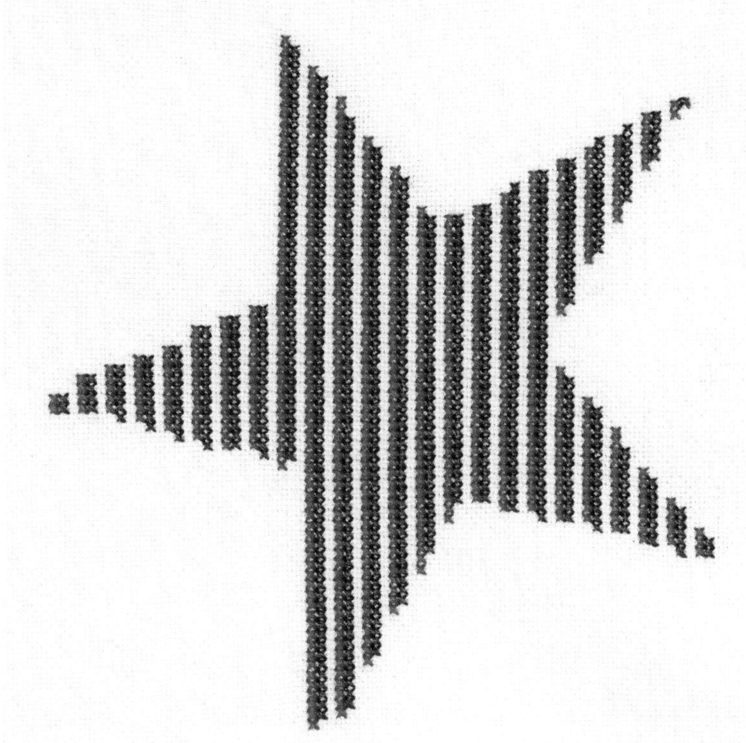

Thread:
DMC 309 Rose, Dark (.2 skeins).

DMC 311 Navy Blue, Medium (.2 skeins).

Stitch count:
71 × 69.

Design shown:
28-count evenweave over 2 threads, 5⅛" × 4⅞" (13 × 12.4 cm).

Fabric amount:
9½" × 9½" (24 × 24 cm).

Other fabrics:
16-count over 1 thread: 4½" × 4⅜" (11.5 × 11.1 cm).
Suggested fabric amount: 9" × 9" (23 × 23 cm).

18-count over 1 thread: 4" × 3⅞" (10 × 9.8 cm).
Suggested fabric amount 8½" × 8½" (21.5 × 21.5 cm).

Legend:

DMC-444

Sunshine

Thread:
DMC 444 Lemon, Dark (.6 skeins).

Stitch count:
70 × 67.

Design shown:
28-count evenweave over 2 threads, 5" × 4¾" (12.5 × 12 cm).

Fabric amount:
9½" × 9½" (24 × 24 cm).

Other fabrics:
16- count over 1 thread: 4⅜" × 4¼" (11.1 × 11 cm). *Suggested fabric amount:* 9" × 8½" (23 × 21.5 cm)

18- count over 1 thread: 3⅞" × 3¾" (9.8 × 9.5 cm). *Suggested fabric amount:* 8½" × 8" (21.5 × 20.5 cm).

HO
ME

WORDS

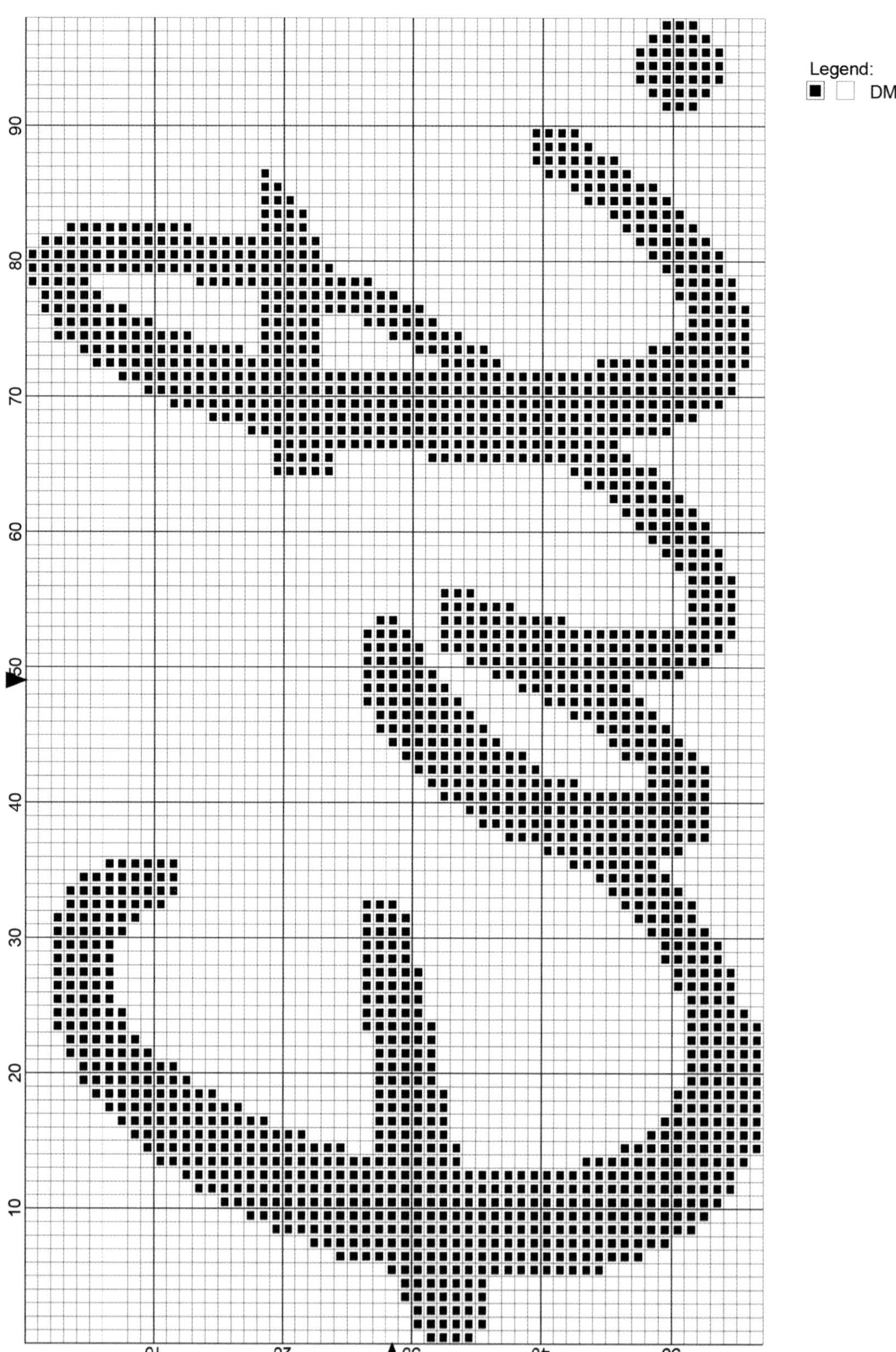

Legend:

DMC-White

Thread:
DMC White (.3 skeins).

Stitch count:
98 × 57.

Design shown:
28-count evenweave over 2 threads,
7" × 4⅛" (18 × 10.5 cm).

Fabric amount:
11½" × 8½" (21.5 × 29 cm).

Other fabrics:
16-count over 1 thread: 6⅛" × 3⅝" (15.5 × 9.2 cm).
Suggested fabric amount: 10½" × 8" (26.5 × 20.5 cm).

18-count over 1 thread: 5½" × 3⅛" (14 × 8 cm).
Suggested fabric amount: 10" × 7½" (25.5 × 19 cm).

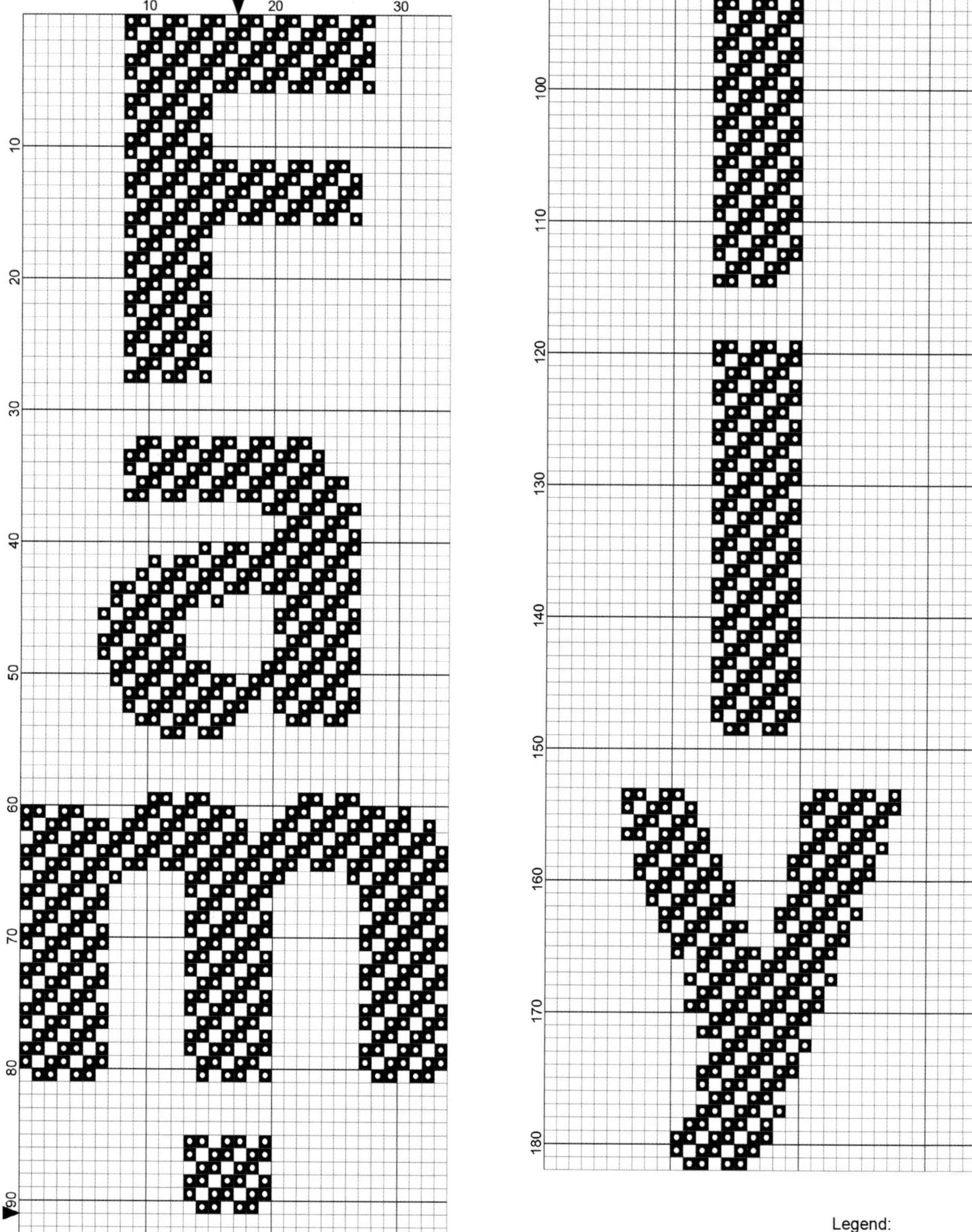

Legend:
DMC-310

Family

Thread:
DMC 310, Black (.5 skeins).

Stitch count:
34 × 182.

Design shown:
28-count evenweave over 2 threads, 2⅜" × 13" (6 × 33 cm).

Fabric amount:
7" × 17½" (18 × 44.5 cm).

Other fabrics:
16-count over 1 thread: 2⅛x 11⅜" (5.4 × 28.8 cm).
Suggested fabric amount: 9" × 12½" (23 × 31.5 cm).

18-count over 1 thread: 1⅞"x 10⅛" (4.8 × 25.7 cm).
Suggested fabric amount: 6½" × 14½" (16.5 × 37 cm).

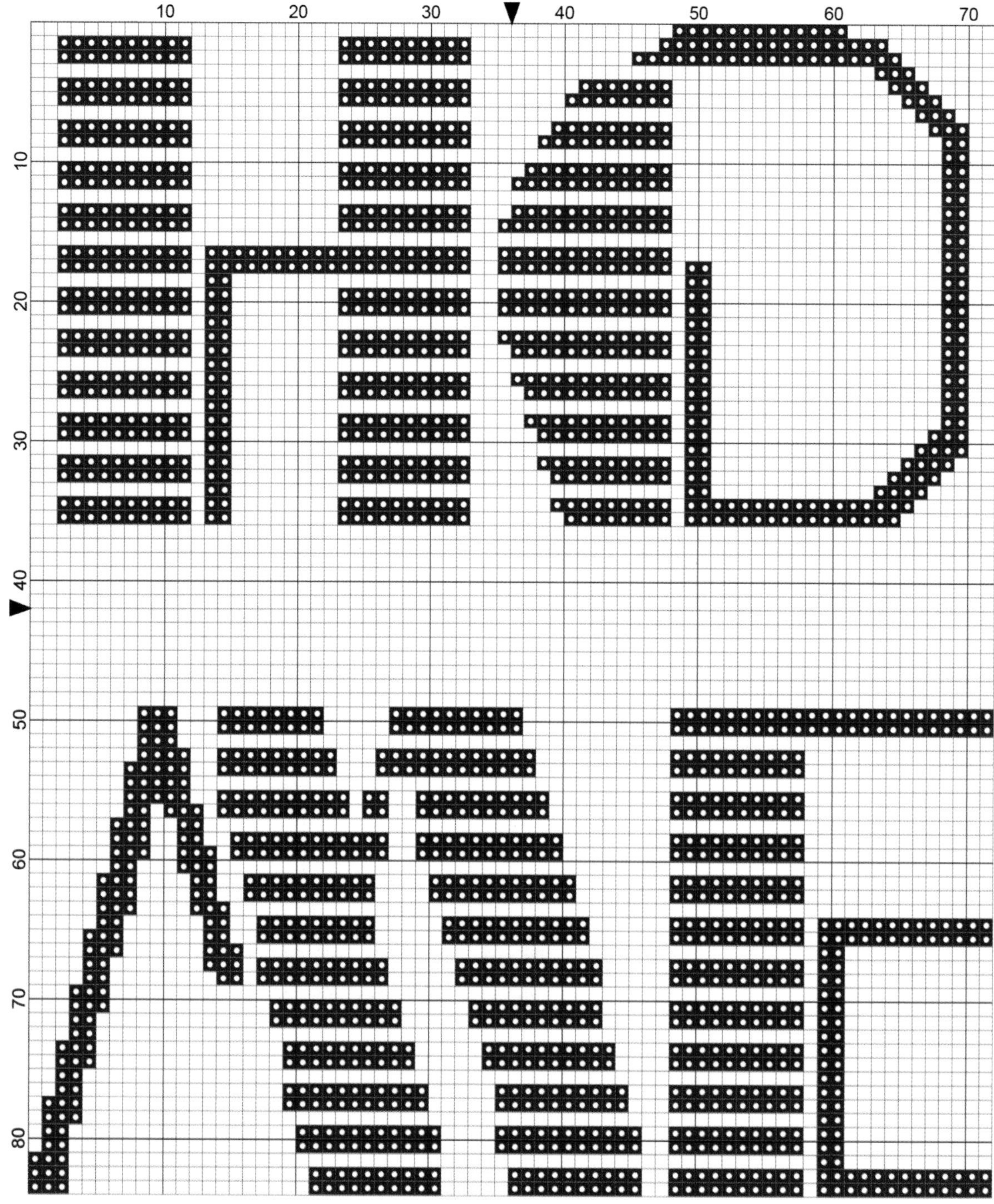

Legend:
DMC-336

Home

Thread:
DMC 336 Navy Blue (.8 skeins).

Stitch count:
72 × 84.

Design shown:
28-count evenweave over 2 threads, 5⅛" × 6" (13 × 15 cm).

Fabric amount:
9½" × 10½" (24 × 26.5 cm).

Other fabrics:
16-count over 1 thread:
4½" × 5¼" (11.5 × 13.5 cm).
Suggested fabric amount:
9" × 10" (23 × 25.5 cm).

18-count over 1 thread:
4" × 4⅝" (10 × 11.7 cm).
Suggested fabric amount:
8½" × 9" (21.5 × 23 cm).

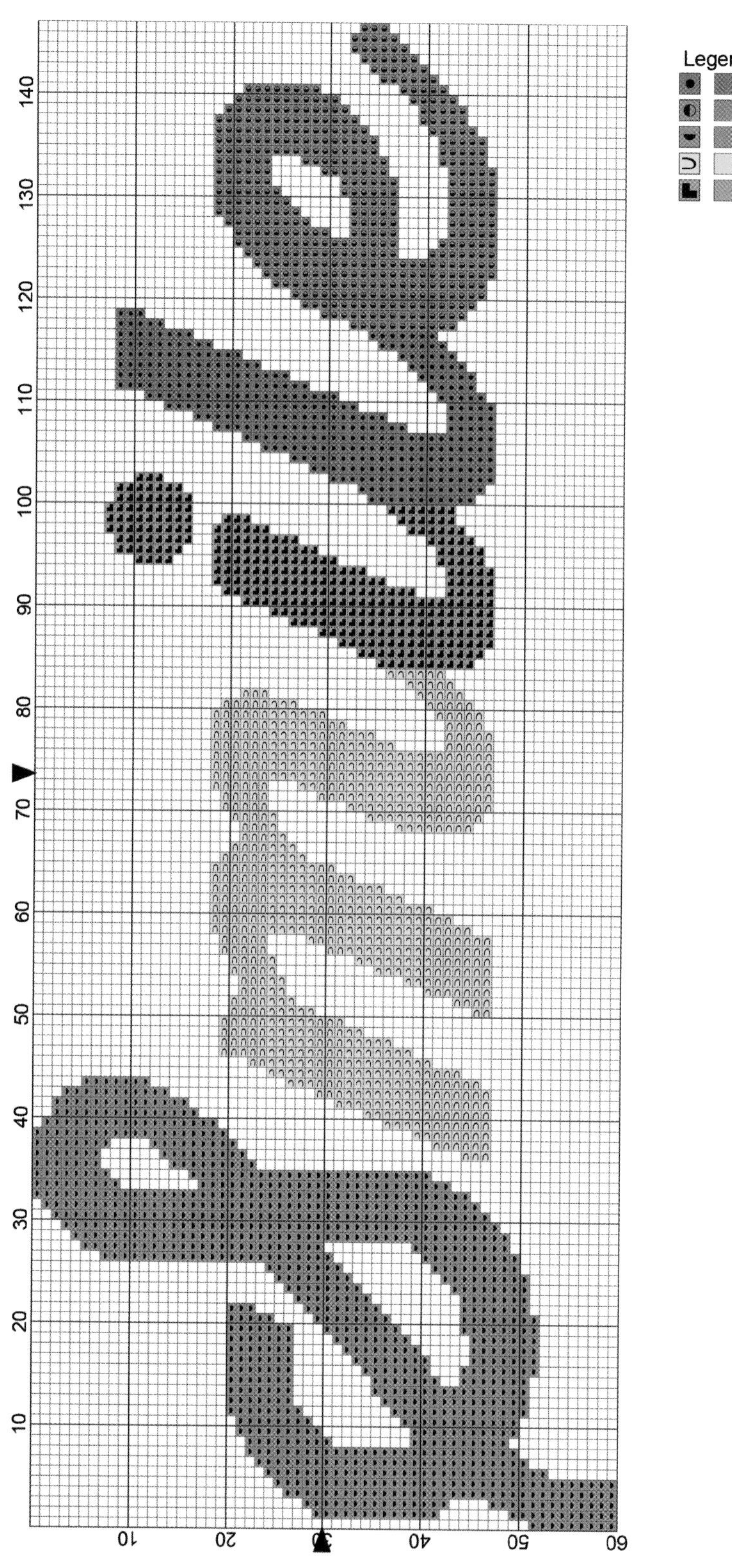

Legend:

- DMC-553
- DMC-602
- DMC-597
- DMC-307
- DMC-320

Smile

Thread:
DMC 553 Violet (.1 skeins).

DMC 602 Cranberry, Medium (.1 skeins).

DMC 597 Turquoise (.2 skeins).

DMC 307 Lemon (.1 skeins).

DMC 320 Pistachio Green, Medium (.1 skeins).

Stitch count:
147 × 60.

Design shown:
28-count evenweave over 2 threads, 10½" × 4¼" (26.5 × 11 cm).

Fabric amount:
15" × 9" (38 × 23 cm).

Other fabrics:
16-count over 1 thread: 9¼" × 3¾" (23.5 × 9.5 cm).
Suggested fabric amount: 13½" × 8" (34.5 × 20.5 cm).

18-count over 1 thread: 8⅛" × 3⅜" (20.6 × 8.6 cm).
Suggested fabric amount: 12¾" × 8⅝" (32.4 × 22 cm)

ABOUT THE AUTHOR

A dual citizen of both the United States and the United Kingdom, Leah Lintz was first introduced to the art of cross-stitching while awaiting the birth of her eldest daughter, and quickly developed a keen eye for the elegant yet simple designs, which she has offered cross-stitching enthusiasts through various platforms such as Etsy. Thousands of her patterns have been purchased by stitchers from over 35 countries. When she's not busy making patterns, making food, or cleaning up after her little (and not so little) people, she loves fair-weather cycling, photographing flowers, knitting, and playing billiards.

MATERIALS

Most of the tools and supplies in this book can be found at your local craft or needlework store. I purchased all of my supplies from Michaels (michaels.com) and Joann Fabrics (joann.com).

Metric Conversion Chart

TO CONVERT	TO:	X BY:
Inches	Centimeters	2.54
Centimeters	Inches	0.4
Feet	Centimeters	30.5
Centimeters	Feet	0.03
Yards	Meters	0.9
Meters	Yards	1.1

ACKNOWLEDGMENTS

To Mike and the kids for putting up with the many, many quick meals I made (read: take-out) and the constant glow of my lamp at 4 in the morning. Thank you guys! Now, Yorkshire pudding for all! Mummy's back!

DEDICATION

I wish to personally thank the following people for making this book possible: Amelia Johanson, Erica Smith, Pamela Norman, Elisabeth Lariviere, and all the staff at F+W. Thank you for keeping me focused and believing that I could get those samples stitched!

A big thank you to Savannah Lintz who used her needle skills to stitch the "Scallop Shell" found in this book.

And last but not least, a huge thank you to my husband and children. You guys enable my addiction to cross-stitch!

Family
Eat.

 Published by Interweave Books, an imprint of F+W Media, Inc., 10151 Carver Road, Suite 200, Blue Ash, Ohio 45242. (800) 289-0963. First Edition.

www.fwcommunity.com

19 18 17 16 15 5 4 3 2 1

Distributed in Canada by Fraser Direct
100 Armstrong Avenue
Georgetown, ON, Canada L7G 5S4
Tel: (905) 877-4411

Distributed in the U.K. and Europe by F&W MEDIA INTERNATIONAL
Brunel House, Newton Abbot, Devon, TQ12 4PU, England
Tel: (+44) 1626 323200,
Fax: (+44) 1626 323319
E-mail: enquiries@fwmedia.com

Distributed in Australia
by Capricorn Link
P.O. Box 704, S. Windsor NSW, 2756 Australia
Tel: (02) 4560 1600, Fax: (02) 4577 5288
E-mail: books@capricornlink.com.au

SRN: 16NW02
ISBN-13: 978-1-63250-453-1

Editorial Director: Kerry Bogert
Acquisitions Editor: Amelia Johanson
Editor: Erica Smith
Art Director: Elisabeth Lariviere
Cover Designer: Frank Rivera and Elisabeth Lariviere
Interior Designer: Pamela Norman